# WRAPPED IN THE CONVERSATION

## TONY E. MEDLEY

**MEDLEY**
PUBLISHING GROUP

A DIVISION OF
TONY E. MEDLEY ENTERPRISES

Medley Publishing Group
drmedley@alcc4me.org

ISBN: 979-8-9934305-0-8 (print)
ISBN: 979-8-9934305-1-5 (ebook)

This book is established to provide information and inspiration to all readers. It is
designed with the understanding that the author is not engaged to render any
psychological, legal, or any other kind of professional advice. The content is the sole
expression of the author. The author is not liable for any physical, psychological,
emotional, financial, or commercial damages, including, but not limited to special,
incidental, consequential, or other damages. All readers are responsible for their own
choices, actions, and results.

*To my family—your love has been a steady*
*reflection of God's faithfulnes…*

*To my church family—your prayers, encouragement,*
*and walk of faith inspire me daily…*

*And to every reader who longs to hear and live by the words*
*God is speaking over your life— may you be forever wrapped in His*
*conversation, strengthened by His promises, and transformed*
*by His unchanging Word…*

Call to Me and I will answer you, and will tell you great and hidden things that you have not known.

JEREMIAH 33:3

# TABLE OF CONTENTS

## PART ONE
## THE FOUNDATIONS OF GOD'S CONVERSATION

# PART TWO
## GOD'S CONVERSATION
## ABOUT YOU

PART THREE
LIVING THE CONVERSATION DAILY

# PREFACE

When I first began writing these words, my heart was not simply to produce another book, but to create a space for you to encounter the living God who still speaks today. Over the years, I have learned that life is not defined by the noise around us but by the voice above us— the eternal voice of God that calls, corrects, encourages, and promises.

This project was born out of prayer, long hours of reflection, and a deep burden to remind the body of Christ that heaven's conversation is not distant. It is active, alive, and personal. Too often, we live as though God has gone silent, when in truth He is speaking through His Word, His Spirit, and His people every single day.

Each chapter in this book represents a facet of that ongoing conversation. You will find Scripture, case studies, prayers, and questions for reflection. These are not meant to be rushed through, but to be sat with—meditated upon, prayed through, and applied in your daily walk.

My prayer is simple: that as you read, you will begin to recognize God's voice more clearly in your own life. That you will see yourself the way heaven sees you—loved, chosen, and called. That you will not only listen to God's conversation but participate in it with faith, obedience, and joy.

This is not just a book of theology or inspiration; it is a companion for your journey of discipleship. May it help you live with confidence that the God who began a good work in you will be faithful to complete it.

Thank you for joining me in this journey. As you turn each page, may you hear heaven's song echoing over your life.

# HOW TO USE THIS BOOK

This book is designed to be a personal and spiritual journey, not a fast read. Take your time. Sit with each chapter. Allow the Holy Spirit to speak to you as you reflect, pray, and listen.

Here's how to get the most out of your time with these pages:

### 1. Pray before you read.
Ask the Holy Spirit to open your heart and reveal what God is saying specifically to you in this season.

### 2. Read intentionally.
Each chapter carries revelation meant to be absorbed, not rushed. Take notes, highlight verses, and record insights that stand out.

### 3. Pray the closing prayers.
Each prayer is a declaration of agreement with heaven's Word over your life. Speak them aloud. Let them become part of your daily devotion.

*4. Engage in the "Discussion & Reflection" section.*
At the end of every chapter, you'll find four or five questions designed to help you pause, process, and apply what you've learned. These questions invite you into deeper thought, honest conversation with God, and practical action steps.

*5. Return often.*
This is not a one-time read; it's a companion for your spiritual growth. Come back to specific chapters whenever you need encouragement, clarity, or a reminder of God's promises.

Whether you use this book in personal study, small group discussion, or devotional time, expect transformation. The more you engage, the clearer God's voice will become.

———————

# INTRODUCTION

This book was born out of prayer, reflection, and a deep conviction that God is still speaking. From Genesis to Revelation, we see a God who communicates—who calls, who promises, who corrects, and who comforts. And if He spoke then, He is surely speaking now. Not just to prophets or apostles, but to ordinary sons and daughters. To you.

My heart in writing these pages is simple: I want you to hear heaven's conversation over your life. Too often, we measure ourselves by the voices of culture, the labels of our past, or the noise of fear. But above it all, there is another voice—the eternal Word of God—declaring that you are loved, chosen, and called.

Each chapter of this book is designed to help you lean in and listen. We will walk through Scripture together. We will look at stories of men and women who trusted God's Word even when circumstances seemed impossible. And at the end of every chapter, you will find a prayer and reflection questions—tools to help you not only learn, but apply, what God is saying.

This book is not meant to be rushed. It is meant to be lived. Take your time. Meditate on the Scriptures. Pray the prayers slowly. Allow God's Spirit to speak personally to you.

I believe with all my heart that if you engage with this book intentionally, you will discover that God has been speaking about your identity, your future, your purpose, and your destiny all along. You will see that you are part of an eternal conversation—one that began before you were born and will continue into eternity.

My prayer is that these words will help you tune your ear to the voice of heaven, and that your life will become an echo of God's promises on earth.

You are loved. You are chosen. You are called. And heaven's conversation is not finished—it's only beginning.

With love and expectation, Dr. Tony E. Medley Sr.

# PART ONE
# THE FOUNDATIONS OF GOD'S CONVERSATION

# CHAPTER 1
# GOD'S ETERNAL WORD OVER YOU

> Forever, O Lord, Your word is settled in heaven.
>
> PSALM 119:89

If you were to strip away everything you know—titles, possessions, even the approval of people—what would remain to anchor your soul? For the child of God, the answer is simple: the eternal Word of God. The psalmist boldly declared, "Forever, O Lord, Your Word is settled in heaven" (Psalm 119:89).

That means the Word of God is not waiting on human agreement, culture's approval, or circumstances to validate it. His Word is established, unshakable, and enduring.

In a world where everything seems to shift—governments rise and fall, economies fluctuate, people come and go—the Word of God remains unchanged. Hebrews 13:8 says, "Jesus Christ is the same yesterday and today and forever." If He is unchanging, then His promises are unchanging.

Think of it like a rock in the middle of a stormy sea. Waves may crash, winds may howl, and boats may be tossed about—but that rock does not move. God's Word is that rock. And when He speaks a word over your life, that word is not subject to expiration dates or human limitations.

## GOD SPOKE BEFORE YOU WERE BORN

Before you ever opened your eyes to this world, God already knew you. More than that—He spoke destiny over your life. Jeremiah 1:5 reveals this profound truth: "Before I formed you in the womb I knew you, before you were born I set you apart; I appointed you as a prophet to the nations."

Notice the order: God knew, He formed, He set apart, He appointed. Your calling didn't begin when you discovered it; it began when God declared it. This means your life is not a random series of events—it is part of a divine script written before time began.

Paul echoes this in Ephesians 1:4: "For He chose us in Him before the creation of the world to be holy and blameless in His sight." Before creation, before Adam and Eve, before sin entered the world, God had already chosen you and spoken a word over you.

That changes how we see ourselves. You are not a mistake. You are not an accident. You are not forgotten. You are chosen, appointed, and sealed by a Word that cannot be broken.

## THE ETERNAL WORD VS. TEMPORARY CIRCUMSTANCES

Paul gives us perspective in 2 Corinthians 4:18: "So we fix our eyes not on what is seen, but on what is unseen, since what is seen is temporary, but what is unseen is eternal."

Everything you see with your physical eyes is temporary. The sickness is temporary. The financial hardship is temporary. The loneliness is temporary. But the Word of God over your life is eternal. It will outlast your trials, your seasons, and even your doubts.

When you face something overwhelming, you can remind yourself:

This may look final, but it is not eternal. God's Word is eternal, and His Word over me will prevail.

## ABRAHAM: PROOF THAT GOD'S WORD PREVAILS

Abraham's life is a master class in trusting God's eternal Word over temporary facts. God promised Abraham descendants as numerous as the stars. But when the promise came, Abraham was nearly 100 years old, and Sarah's womb was barren. From every human perspective, the promise was impossible.

Romans 4:19–21 paints the picture: "Without weakening in his faith, he faced the fact that his body was as good as dead—since he was about a hundred years old—and that Sarah's womb was also dead. Yet he did not waver through unbelief regarding the promise of God but was strengthened in his faith and gave glory to God, being fully persuaded that God had power to do what he had promised."

Notice the detail: Abraham did not deny the facts. He faced them. Faith is not pretending problems do not exist—it is believing they do not have the final say. Abraham held onto God's eternal Word, and that Word prevailed.

The same God who fulfilled His Word for Abraham will fulfill His Word for you.

## MARY: THE WORD MADE FLESH

Fast-forward centuries later to a young girl named Mary. When the angel announced that she would give birth to the Son of God, she asked, "How will this be, since I am a virgin?" (Luke 1:34). The answer was simple yet profound:

"For no word from God will ever fail" (Luke 1:37, NIV).

Mary did not have to figure out how. She simply had to believe Who. God's eternal Word had the power within itself to bring itself to pass.

Mary responded with humility: "May it be to me according to your word" (Luke 1:38). That is the posture God calls us to take.

## JOSEPH: FROM PIT TO PALACE

Joseph received a dream as a teenager—a dream that he would one day lead and preserve his family. But almost immediately, his life seemed to move in the opposite direction. Betrayed by his brothers, thrown into a pit, sold into slavery, and imprisoned unjustly, Joseph's circumstances looked nothing like his calling.

Yet the Word of God sustained him. Psalm 105:19 says, "Until the time came to fulfill his dreams, the Lord tested Joseph's character." In the hidden places of suffering, God was shaping Joseph into the man who could carry the weight of the promise.

The eternal Word over Joseph's life prevailed. He rose to power in Egypt, and the very brothers who had betrayed him bowed before him in fulfillment of his dream.

## DAVID: ANOINTED BUT NOT YET APPOINTED

David's story is another illustration of the eternal Word at work. As a shepherd boy, he was anointed king by Samuel. Yet instead of ascending to the throne immediately, David spent years running for his life, hiding in caves, and enduring betrayal.

The Word was true, but the timing required trust. David learned to strengthen himself in the Lord (1 Samuel 30:6) because God's Word had to sustain him through delay and danger.

When the time came, God fulfilled His Word, and David became king over Israel.

## JESUS: THE LIVING WORD

Ultimately, every promise of God finds its "yes" in Jesus Christ (2 Corinthians 1:20). He is the living Word (John 1:1, 14). His life, death, and resurrection prove beyond doubt that God's Word cannot be defeated.

Even the cross—the darkest moment in history—was not the end. The Word that declared, "On the third day He will rise again," came to pass. If death itself could not silence God's Word, nothing in your life can silence it either.

## HOLDING FAST IN THE WAITING

Waiting is often the hardest part of faith. The gap between promise and fulfillment tests us. But remember: delay is not denial. God's eternal Word is still working.

Seeds do not sprout the moment they are planted. They grow underground, in the unseen, until the appointed time. The same is true with God's Word over your life.

Galatians 6:9 encourages us: "Let us not become weary in doing good, for at the proper time we will reap a harvest if we do not give up."

## HOW TO ALIGN WITH GOD'S WORD

1. *Confess It Daily*—Speak God's promises aloud. Your words align your heart with His truth.
2. *Meditate on It*—Fill your mind with Scripture. Joshua 1:8 says success comes from meditating on God's Word day and night.
3. *Pray His Word*—Use His promises as your prayer language. Remind God of what He has spoken.
4. *Worship Through It*—Worship is declaring, "Lord, You are greater than what I see."
5. *Walk in Community*—Surround yourself with people who reinforce God's truth, not the enemy's lies.

## THE BATTLE OF COMPETING VOICES

Every believer faces a battle of voices:

- Enemy: "You are forgotten."
- **God: "I will never leave you nor forsake you." (Hebrews 13:5)**

- Fear: "This will destroy you."
- **God: "No weapon formed against you shall prosper." (Isaiah 54:17)**

- Doubt: "It is too late."
- **God: "I make all things new." (Revelation 21:5)**

Your victory comes by choosing which voice you believe.

## WHEN THE WORD SEEMS SILENT

What about when nothing seems to change—when you pray, declare, and believe, but life stays the same?

Remember Joseph in prison. Remember David in caves. Remember Jesus in the tomb. The silence does not mean God's Word has failed—it means God's timing is still unfolding. Faith is not only trusting God when He speaks but also trusting Him when He seems silent.

## PRAYER

Father, thank You that Your Word over my life is eternal and unshakable. I choose to align myself with what You have spoken. I declare that every promise You have made will come to pass in my life. Teach me to wait with faith, to fight with Your Word, and to stand when everything around me says otherwise. In Jesus' name, amen.

## DISCUSSION & REFLECTION

1. Which promises from Scripture speak most directly to your life right now?

_____

_____

_____

_____

_____

_____

_____

_____

2. How have you seen God's Word prevail over circumstances in your past?

_____

_____

_____

_____

_____

_____

_____

_____

3. What voices tend to compete with God's Word in your mind, and how can you silence them?

_____

_____

_____

_____

_____

_____

_____

4. What daily practices help you keep God's promises before you?

_____

_____

_____

_____

_____

_____

_____

_____

_____

5. Where do you need to shift from fear to faith today?

_____

_____

_____

_____

_____

_____

_____

_____

# CHAPTER 2
# JESUS, THE MEDIATOR
# OF THE CONVERSATION

> In the beginning was the Word, and the Word was with God, and the Word was God.
>
> JOHN 1:1

**B**efore there was a written Bible, before there were prophets or apostles, there was the Living Word—Jesus Christ Himself. John's Gospel opens with a breathtaking truth: "In the beginning was the Word, and the Word was with God, and the Word was God."

The Word was not just spoken—it was embodied. Jesus is the eternal Word wrapped in human flesh, the perfect revelation of God's heart. If you want to know what God is saying, you need only look at Jesus.

Hebrews 1:1–2 confirms this: "In the past God spoke to our ancestors through the prophets at many times and in various ways, but in these last days He has spoken to us by His Son."

Every miracle, every teaching, every action of Jesus is God's conversation with humanity.

## THE MEDIATOR OF HEAVEN AND EARTH

A mediator is someone who stands between two parties to reconcile them, to bridge the gap, and to make understanding possible. Humanity was separated from God by sin, unable to cross the chasm. But Jesus came as our Mediator.

1 Timothy 2:5 says it plainly: "For there is one God and one Mediator between God and mankind, the man Christ Jesus."

Jesus does not merely represent us to the Father; He also reveals the Father to us. He is the bridge, the go-between, the translator of heaven's heart into human understanding.

## JESUS THE INTERCESSOR

Hebrews 7:25 gives us another glimpse into His role: "Therefore He is able to save completely those who come to God through Him, because He always lives to intercede for them."

Think about this: right now, in this very moment, Jesus is interceding for you. He is not distant or silent. He is speaking your name before the Father, covering you in His prayers, and advocating for your destiny.

When you feel unseen or unheard, remember that Jesus is presenting your life before the throne of God. His intercession ensures that heaven's purposes prevail over your earthly struggles.

## ILLUSTRATION: THE TRANSLATOR

Imagine two people trying to communicate—one speaks English, the other speaks only Mandarin. They may sit in the same room, but without a translator, they cannot understand each other.

That is what Jesus does for us. He translates the heart of the Father into a language we can understand. When we read His parables, witness His compassion, and see His sacrifice on the cross, we are hearing the Father's voice clearly.

At the same time, Jesus takes our broken prayers, our stumbling words, and our limited understanding and presents them perfectly to the Father. Even when all we can say is, "Lord, help me," Jesus carries that cry to heaven's throne.

## JESUS CLARIFIES THE FATHER'S HEART

The disciples once asked Jesus, "Show us the Father." Jesus replied, "Anyone who has seen Me has seen the Father" (John 14:9).

When you see Jesus touching lepers, you see the Father's compassion. When you hear Jesus forgiving sinners, you hear the Father's mercy. When you watch Jesus calming storms, you witness the Father's authority.

Jesus is not just the Mediator of words—He is the Mediator of God's heart. He does not simply tell us about God; He embodies Him.

## CASE STUDY: THE WOMAN AT THE WELL

In John 4, Jesus meets a Samaritan woman at a well. Culturally, politically, and morally, she was an outcast. Yet Jesus sat with her, spoke truth, and revealed living water that could satisfy her soul.

Through this conversation, Jesus revealed the Father's heart: "God is spirit, and His worshipers must worship in the Spirit and in truth" (John 4:24). He took what was distant, misunderstood, and clouded by religion and made it clear, personal, and life-giving.

This is what Jesus still does for us. He makes the Father's heart accessible.

## JESUS' INTERCESSION AND OUR PRAYER LIFE

Because Jesus is our Mediator, prayer is no longer a desperate attempt to reach a distant God. Instead, it is an ongoing dialogue with the Father through the Son.

- We pray in Jesus' name because He is the One who grants us access.

- We pray with confidence because Jesus has already bridged the gap.
- We pray with hope because He is interceding for us continually.

Romans 8:34 reminds us: "Christ Jesus, who died—more than that, who was raised to life—is at the right hand of God and is also interceding for us."

This means your prayers are never alone. Jesus amplifies them, perfects them, and presents them to the Father with His own authority.

## PRACTICAL WAYS TO LISTEN TO JESUS' MEDIATION

1. *Read His Words in the Gospels*—Every red-letter word is God's heart translated for you.
2. *Follow His Example*—How Jesus lived is how heaven looks on earth.
3. *Listen in Prayer*—Ask Jesus, "What are You praying over me right now? "
4. *Trust His Advocacy*—Rest knowing He is representing you before the Father.
5. *Obey Promptly*—When He makes the Father's will clear, walk in it immediately.

## WHEN HAS CHRIST CLARIFIED GOD'S HEART?

There are moments in every believer's life when Jesus makes God's heart unmistakably clear:

- In a time of grief, you experience peace that does not make sense.
- In confusion, His Word leaps off the page with clarity.
- In failure, you sense forgiveness instead of condemnation.

These moments are the fruit of Jesus' mediating work. He takes the Father's eternal truth and brings it into your personal situation.

## PRAYER

Lord Jesus, thank You for being my Mediator. Thank You for bridging the gap between me and the Father. Help me to listen to Your voice above all others and to trust that You are always interceding for me. May my prayers rise with confidence, knowing they are carried by You into the Father's presence. Amen.

## DISCUSSION & REFLECTION

1. How does knowing that Jesus intercedes for you change your prayer life?

_____

_____

_____

_____

_____

2. What areas of your life do you need to entrust more fully to His intercession?

_____

_____

_____

_____

_____

3. When has Christ clarified God's heart for you in a personal way?

_____

_____

_____

_____

_____

4. How can you better listen for Jesus' "translation" of the Father's will in your daily walk?

_____

_____

_____

_____

_____

_____

# CHAPTER 3
# THE ROLE OF THE HOLY SPIRIT IN REVEALING GOD'S THOUGHTS

> These are the things God has revealed to us by His Spirit. The Spirit searches all things, even the deep things of God.

> 1 CORINTHIANS 2:10

The Holy Spirit is not an optional addition to the Christian life—He is essential. Without the Spirit, we cannot truly understand God's heart or walk in His ways. Paul tells us that the Spirit "searches the deep things of God" (1 Corinthians 2:10). This means the Spirit has access to the very thoughts of God and chooses to share them with us.

The Spirit is not distant; He is the indwelling presence of God, given to every believer. Jesus promised in John 14:26: "But the Advocate, the Holy Spirit, whom the Father will send in My name, will teach you all things and will remind you of everything I have said to you." He is our divine Teacher, Interpreter, and Comforter.

## THE SPIRIT REVEALS TRUTH

When Jesus spoke of the Holy Spirit, He described Him as the "Spirit of truth." John 16:13 says: "But when He, the Spirit of truth, comes, He will guide you into all the truth. He will not speak on His own; He will speak only what He hears, and He will tell you what is yet to come."

This is more than intellectual understanding. The Spirit does not just give us facts about God; He gives us revelation. Revelation is truth that transforms. It is when Scripture suddenly becomes alive, when God's whisper breaks into your prayer time, when wisdom comes in the exact moment you need it.

## ILLUSTRATION: THE HIKING GUIDE

Imagine you are on a hike through a dense forest. The path is unfamiliar, the terrain is tricky, and the possibility of getting lost is real. Now imagine you have an experienced guide—someone who knows every trail, every landmark, and every hidden danger.

That is what the Holy Spirit does. He leads us through the complexities of life, pointing out the safe paths, warning us of pitfalls, and ensuring that we reach the destination God has prepared. Left to ourselves, we wander; with the Spirit, we walk in wisdom.

## THE SPIRIT AS COMFORTER

Jesus described the Spirit as *Parakletos*—the Helper, Comforter, or Advocate. In moments of grief, discouragement, or fear, it is the Spirit who comes alongside us to strengthen and encourage.

Romans 8:26 reminds us: "In the same way, the Spirit helps us in our weakness. We do not know what we ought to pray for, but the Spirit Himself intercedes for us through wordless groans." Even when you cannot find words, the Spirit translates your heart's cries into prayers that reach the throne of God.

## CASE STUDY: PHILIP AND THE ETHIOPIAN EUNUCH

In Acts 8, we see the Spirit at work as a guide. Philip is told by an angel to go to a desert road. Once there, the Spirit directs him to approach a chariot where an Ethiopian official is reading Isaiah. Philip explains the Scripture and shares Jesus, and the man is baptized.

Without the Spirit's guidance, this divine appointment would never have happened. The Spirit orchestrated the timing, the location, and the conversation. This is how He still works in our lives—arranging moments where heaven touches earth.

## CASE STUDY: PAUL'S MISSIONARY JOURNEYS

The book of Acts also shows how the Spirit directs our steps in surprising ways. In Acts 16, Paul and his companions are "kept by the Holy Spirit from preaching the word in the province of Asia." Instead, Paul has a vision of a man in Macedonia asking for help. That vision redirected the course of the gospel into Europe.

The Spirit's guidance is not always about where to go—it is sometimes about where not to go. He sees the bigger picture and positions us for fruitfulness.

## HEARING THE SPIRIT'S VOICE

Many believers ask, "How do I know if it is the Spirit speaking? " While God can speak in many ways—through Scripture, circumstances, inner impressions, or wise counsel—the Spirit's voice always carries certain characteristics:

- It aligns with Scripture.
- It brings peace, not confusion.
- It glorifies Jesus, not self.
- It produces fruit consistent with God's character (Galatians 5:22–23).

Learning to hear the Spirit is like learning to recognize a familiar voice. The more time you spend with Him, the clearer His whispers become.

## PRACTICAL WAYS TO WALK WITH THE SPIRIT

1. *Daily Surrender*—Begin each day with, "Holy Spirit, lead me today."
2. *Scripture Saturation*—The Spirit uses the Word to guide you. Read it prayerfully.
3. *Stillness*—Create space in your day to listen, not just talk.
4. *Obedience*—When you sense His prompting, act on it. Obedience sharpens your ear.
5. *Community Discernment*—The Spirit also speaks through trusted believers who confirm His leading.

## RESISTING THE SPIRIT

Scripture also warns us that we can grieve (Ephesians 4:30), resist (Acts 7:51), or quench (1 Thessalonians 5:19) the Spirit. This happens when we ignore His promptings, cling to sin, or drown out His voice with distractions.

If you feel distant from the Spirit, the solution is not striving but surrender. Simply pray, "Holy Spirit, I repent for ignoring You. Speak again—I am listening."

## THE SPIRIT AND THE MIND OF CHRIST

Paul concludes in 1 Corinthians 2:16: "But we have the mind of Christ." How? Through the Spirit, who reveals God's thoughts to us. This means you are not left to figure out life on your own. The wisdom of heaven is available to you through the Spirit's presence.

This is a staggering truth: the very Spirit who knows God's

thoughts now dwells in you, guiding, shaping, and empowering your journey.

## PRAYER

Holy Spirit, open my ears to hear You clearly. Search the deep things of God and reveal His heart to me. Guide my steps, comfort me in weakness, and lead me closer to Jesus every day. Give me wisdom to walk in Your path and courage to obey Your promptings. Amen.

## DISCUSSION & REFLECTION

1. How have you experienced the Spirit's guidance in your life?

_____

_____

_____

_____

_____

_____

2. What helps you tune in to His voice amid the noise of daily life?

_____

_____

_____

_____

_____

_____

3. Are there areas where you have resisted the Spirit's leading? How can you realign today?

_____

_____

_____

_____

_____

_____

4. What new practices could you adopt to grow more sensitive to His direction?

_____

_____

_____

_____

# CHAPTER 4

# ANGELS AND WITNESSES IN THE HEAVENLY DIALOGUE

> Are not all angels ministering spirits sent to serve those who will inherit salvation?
>
> HEBREWS 1:14

**M**any believers live unaware of the constant activity of heaven on their behalf. Yet Scripture is clear: angels are part of God's ongoing work in our lives. They are not distant, passive observers; they are sent with assignments—to protect, to deliver, to minister, and to carry out God's purposes.

Hebrews 1:14 describes them as "ministering spirits." Their ministry is not general; it is directed toward you, an heir of salvation. Angels are woven into God's eternal conversation, responding to His commands and serving His people.

## ANGELS AS MESSENGERS

Throughout Scripture, angels appear as messengers, delivering heaven's words to earth. Gabriel announced to Mary that she would bear the Messiah (Luke 1:26–38). Angels came to Joseph in dreams to guide and protect Jesus' early life (Matthew 1:20; 2:13). They appeared at Jesus' resurrection, declaring the good news that He had risen (Luke 24:6–7).

Their very name, *angelos*, means "messenger." They are carriers of God's voice, ensuring that His words are communicated, confirmed, and carried out.

## ANGELS AS PROTECTORS

Psalm 91:11–12 gives us a stunning promise: "For He will command His angels concerning you to guard you in all your ways; they will lift you up in their hands so that you will not strike your foot against a stone."

Angels are not decorative figures in Bible stories—they are active protectors. Whether seen or unseen, their assignment includes guarding you from harm as you walk in God's will.

## ILLUSTRATION: PETER'S MIRACULOUS RESCUE

In Acts 12, Peter was imprisoned by Herod, chained between guards, awaiting execution. But the church prayed earnestly, and heaven responded: "Suddenly an angel of the Lord appeared and a light shone in the cell. He struck Peter on the side and woke him up. 'Quick, get up! ' he said, and the chains fell off Peter's wrists" (Acts 12:7).

The angel led Peter past guards, through iron gates, and into freedom. This was not a symbolic story—it was a real intervention. Heaven acted in direct response to prayer, sending an angel to shift the course of history.

If God dispatched angels for Peter, can you believe He is still sending angels for you?

## THE WITNESSES OF HEAVEN

Hebrews 12:1 adds another dimension: "Therefore, since we are surrounded by such a great cloud of witnesses, let us throw off everything that hinders and the sin that so easily entangles."

This "cloud of witnesses" refers to the faithful saints who have gone before us, whose lives now testify to God's power. They are not passive; their stories, their victories, and their faith surround us like an arena of encouragement.

Imagine running a marathon through a stadium filled with those who have finished their race. With every step you take, they cheer with their lives: "If God sustained us, He will sustain you too."

## CASE STUDY: ELISHA AND THE HEAVENLY ARMY

In 2 Kings 6, Elisha and his servant were surrounded by an enemy army. The servant panicked, but Elisha prayed, "Open his eyes, Lord, so that he may see" (v. 17). Suddenly, the servant's eyes were opened, and he saw hills full of horses and chariots of fire surrounding Elisha.

The reality had not changed—but his awareness had. The heavenly host had been there all along, ready to defend.

So it is with you. Even when you feel outnumbered, heaven's forces are present.

## ANGELS IN JESUS' LIFE

Angels played a significant role throughout Jesus' ministry:

- At His birth: They announced His arrival to shepherds (Luke 2:13–14).
- After His temptation: They came to minister to Him (Matthew 4:11).
- In Gethsemane: An angel strengthened Him as He prepared for the cross (Luke 22:43).
- At His resurrection: They declared His victory over death (Matthew 28:2–6).

If Jesus, the Son of God, was ministered to by angels, how much more can we expect their ministry as heirs of salvation?

## ANGELS AND PRAYER

One of the ways angels participate in the heavenly dialogue is by responding to prayer. In Daniel 10, an angel tells Daniel that his prayer was heard from the first day, but spiritual opposition delayed the answer. The angel came as a direct response to Daniel's persistence in prayer.

This shows us that prayer is not just words spoken into the air—it is participation in heaven's activity. Your prayers move angels into action.

## PRACTICAL WAYS TO LIVE AWARE OF HEAVEN'S HELP

1. *Pray with Expectation*—Believe that heaven is listening and responding.
2. *Rest in God's Protection*—Trust that angels guard your path even when unseen.
3. *Ask for Discernment*—Pray for spiritual eyes to see God's activity.
4. *Live with Courage*—Knowing heaven fights for you should silence fear.
5. *Stay in God's Will*—Angels are sent to serve those walking in obedience

## ENCOURAGEMENT FROM HEAVEN'S INVESTMENT

You are not alone in your journey of faith. Heaven is invested in your story. Angels are dispatched, witnesses surround you, and the Spirit testifies within you. Together, they form a chorus that says, "God's Word over you will not fail."

Let this truth strengthen you in times of discouragement. When you feel isolated, remember that heaven's courtroom is actively engaged in your destiny.

## PRAYER

Father, thank You for sending angels to serve Your purposes in my life. Open my eyes to recognize Your hand at work through heavenly help. Thank You for the witnesses who testify to Your faithfulness and remind me that I am not alone. Strengthen me with the courage to walk in the assurance of heaven's investment. Amen.

## DISCUSSION & REFLECTION

1. When have you experienced God's protection in a way you could not explain?

_____

_____

_____

_____

_____

2. How does knowing that angels are sent to serve you encourage your faith?

_____

_____

_____

_____

_____

3. What does the "cloud of witnesses" mean for your daily walk with Christ?

_____

_____

_____

_____

_____

4. How can you pray differently, knowing heaven responds to your prayers?

_____

_____

_____

_____

_____

# CHAPTER 5
# SCRIPTURE AS THE RECORD OF HEAVEN'S CONVERSATION

> For the word of God is alive and active. Sharper than any double-edged sword, it penetrates even to dividing soul and spirit, joints and marrow; it judges the thoughts and attitudes of the heart.
>
> HEBREWS 4:12

W hen we open the Bible, we are not simply reading ink on paper—we are hearing heaven's voice in written form. Scripture is not dead history; it is the living record of God's eternal conversation with His people. It records His promises, His purposes, His warnings, and His encouragement.

This is why Hebrews 4:12 describes the Word as "alive and active." Unlike any other book, the Bible breathes with the Spirit of God. It has the power to cut through confusion, reveal truth, and transform hearts.

When you hold a Bible in your hands, you are holding the written confirmation of heaven's thoughts toward you.

## THE WORD ANCHORS US

In a world of shifting values, cultural noise, and personal uncertainty, the Word of God is the anchor. Anchors are designed to keep ships steady in the storm. Scripture holds us firm when winds of doubt, temptation, or suffering try to carry us away.

Psalm 119:105 says, "Your word is a lamp to my feet and a light to my path." Without it, we stumble in darkness. With it, we can walk steadily, guided by the light of heaven's truth.

## JESUS AND THE POWER OF "IT IS WRITTEN"

One of the most powerful demonstrations of Scripture's role comes from Jesus Himself. In Matthew 4:1–11, He was led into the wilderness to be tempted by the devil. Each temptation struck at His identity, His mission, and His trust in the Father.

But Jesus did not argue, negotiate, or philosophize. He simply declared:

- "It is written: Man shall not live on bread alone, but on every word that comes from the mouth of God" (v. 4).
- "It is also written: Do not put the Lord your God to the test" (v. 7).
- "Away from me, Satan! For it is written: Worship the Lord your God, and serve Him only" (v. 10).

Three times, Jesus resisted with "It is written." Scripture was His shield, His sword, and His anchor.

If the Son of God used the written Word to resist temptation, how much more should we?

## SCRIPTURE AS A WEAPON

Ephesians 6:17 calls the Word of God "the sword of the Spirit." A sword is both defensive and offensive. With it, we defend ourselves against lies, and we also strike down the schemes of the enemy.

When fear whispers, Scripture answers.
When doubt rises, Scripture declares truth.
When temptation entices, Scripture cuts it off.

The enemy fears a believer who knows the Word, because Scripture is not opinion—it is divine authority.

## CASE STUDY: THE BEREANS

In Acts 17:11, the Bereans are described as "more noble" because they "examined the Scriptures every day to see if what Paul said was true." They did not just take words at face value—they measured everything against God's record.

This shows us that Scripture is the ultimate filter. It protects us from deception, grounds us in truth, and ensures that what we hear aligns with heaven's conversation.

## THE LIVING WORD AND THE WRITTEN WORD

It is important to remember that Jesus is the Living Word, and the Bible is the written Word. The two are inseparable. The Spirit illuminates Scripture so that through it we encounter Christ Himself.

John 5:39–40 captures this balance. Jesus said: "You study the Scriptures diligently because you think that in them you have eternal life. These are the very Scriptures that testify about Me, yet you refuse to come to Me to have life."

The goal is not to simply know verses—it is to know the God those verses reveal.

## SCRIPTURE SHAPES OUR IDENTITY

The Bible not only reveals who God is—it reveals who we are in Him. It tells us:

- We are children of God (John 1:12).
- We are new creations (2 Corinthians 5:17).
- We are more than conquerors (Romans 8:37).
- We are seated with Christ in heavenly places (Ephesians 2:6).

When the world tries to define us by our failures, backgrounds, or mistakes, Scripture redefines us by heaven's perspective.

## THE WORD AS DAILY BREAD

Jesus said in Matthew 4:4: "Man shall not live on bread alone, but on every word that comes from the mouth of God." Just as our physical bodies need daily nourishment, our spirits need the daily sustenance of the Word.

Neglecting Scripture starves our faith. Feeding on it strengthens us to endure, resist, and grow.

Think of the Bible not as a book to occasionally reference but as daily bread to consume, digest, and live by.

## PRACTICAL WAYS TO ENGAGE SCRIPTURE

1. *Read Daily*—Make time every day, even if short, to read Scripture.
2. *Meditate Deeply*—Choose a verse or passage and reflect on it throughout your day.
3. *Memorize Intentionally*—Store Scripture in your heart to draw on in times of need.

4. *Pray the Word*—Turn verses into prayers. For example: "Lord, be my shepherd today."

5. *Apply Obediently*—The power of Scripture is unlocked when we live it, not just know it.

## WHEN SCRIPTURE BECOMES PERSONAL

There are moments when the Word leaps off the page and speaks directly to your situation. This is the Spirit breathing life into the text.

- In grief, Psalm 34:18 says, "The Lord is close to the brokenhearted."
- In fear, Isaiah 41:10 declares, "Do not fear, for I am with you."
- In uncertainty, Proverbs 3:5–6 reminds us, "Trust in the Lord with all your heart."

These verses become anchors, holding us steady when everything else shakes.

## SCRIPTURE AS THE FINAL AUTHORITY

In a time when opinions are loud and truth seems relative, Scripture remains the ultimate authority. Isaiah 40:8 says, "The grass withers and the flowers fall, but the word of our God endures forever."

When culture shifts, the Word stands. When philosophies change, the Word endures. When feelings fluctuate, the Word remains.

To live anchored in the Bible is to live anchored in heaven's eternal record.

## PRAYER

Lord, thank You for Your Word. Thank You that it is living, active, and sharper than any sword. Help me to meditate on it daily, to apply it faithfully, and to wield it boldly in the face of temptation and trial. May Your Word anchor me in every season of life. Amen.

———————

## DISCUSSION & REFLECTION

1. How does viewing Scripture as heaven's record change your approach to reading the Bible?

_____

_____

_____

_____

_____

2. What verses have become anchors for you in difficult times?

_____

_____

_____

_____

_____

_____

3. How can you incorporate Scripture more intentionally into your daily routine?

_____

_____

_____

_____

_____

_____

4. In what areas of your life do you need to declare, "It is written?"

_____

_____

_____

_____

_____

_____

# PART TWO
# GOD'S CONVERSATION
# ABOUT YOU

# CHAPTER 6
# GOD'S CONVERSATION ABOUT YOUR IDENTITY

> But you are a chosen people, a royal priesthood, a holy nation, God's special possession, that you may declare the praises of Him who called you out of darkness into His wonderful light.
>
> 1 PETER 2:9

Every human being wrestles with the question: Who am I? Culture tries to answer: *You are what you achieve. You are what you look like. You are what people think of you.*

The enemy whispers: *You are your failures. You are your past. You are unworthy.*

But God has a different word. His eternal declaration over you is not based on shifting opinions, circumstances, or history. Your identity is not earned—it is received. You are defined not by what you do but by Whose you are.

## GOD'S DECLARATION OVER YOU

Through Scripture, God speaks identity into His children:

- *Chosen:* "You did not choose Me, but I chose you" (John 15:16).
- *Beloved:* "I have loved you with an everlasting love" (Jeremiah 31:3).
- *Redeemed:* "In Him we have redemption through His blood" (Ephesians 1:7).
- *Child of God:* "See what great love the Father has lavished on us, that we should be called children of God! " (1 John 3:1).

The world may label you one way, but heaven calls you something else.

## IDENTITY IS RECEIVED, NOT EARNED

Religion often whispers that you must earn your way into God's favor. But the gospel declares identity as a gift. Just as a baby does nothing to earn the name of a family, you did nothing to earn being called a child of God.

Ephesians 2:8–9 reminds us: "For it is by grace you have been saved, through faith—and this is not from yourselves, it is the gift of God—not by works, so that no one can boast."

Your identity is not wages for performance—it is inheritance by grace.

## CASE STUDY: GIDEON

When the angel of the Lord appeared to Gideon in Judges 6, he called him a "mighty warrior." At that moment, Gideon was hiding in fear, threshing wheat in a winepress. His circumstances said *coward.* His family background said *insignificant.* But heaven's conversation said *mighty.*

God was not speaking to Gideon's present condition. He was speaking to his eternal identity. The same is true for you. God calls you according to His plan, not your past.

## CASE STUDY: SIMON PETER

Simon was impulsive, unstable, and often inconsistent. Yet Jesus declared, "You are Peter, and on this rock I will build My church" (Matthew 16:18).

Jesus spoke identity before Peter lived it out. Even after Peter denied Him three times, Jesus restored him with three affirmations of love (John 21:15–17).

Your failures do not erase God's identity over you. His Word stands stronger than your weakness.

## CASE STUDY: THE PRODIGAL SON

In Luke 15, the prodigal rehearsed a speech of shame: "I am no longer worthy to be called your son." But when the father saw him, he ran, embraced him, and clothed him with a robe, ring, and sandals.

The father never called him a servant. He called him *son*.

This is the Father's heart: no matter how far you have run, your identity as His child remains intact.

## FALSE LABELS GOD REMOVES

Many carry labels not given by God:

- Failure
- Rejected
- Unworthy
- Unlovable
- Forgotten

But when God speaks, these labels are replaced:

- From failure to more than a conqueror (Romans 8:37)
- From rejected to chosen (Ephesians 1:4)
- From unworthy to redeemed (1 Corinthians 6:20)
- From unlovable to beloved (Romans 8:38–39)
- From forgotten to engraved on His hands (Isaiah 49:16)

## LIVING FROM IDENTITY, NOT FOR IDENTITY

One of the greatest shifts in the Christian life is moving from striving for identity to living from identity.

- You do not obey to become a child—you obey because you are a child.
- You do not serve to earn God's love—you serve because you already have His love.
- You do not fight for victory—you fight from victory secured in Christ.

When you live from identity, your actions flow out of security, not insecurity.

## PRACTICAL STEPS TO EMBRACE IDENTITY

1. *Declare It Daily*—Speak God's words over yourself: "I am chosen, beloved, and redeemed."
2. *Replace Lies with Truth*—When shame rises, confront it with Scripture.
3. *Surround Yourself with Reminders*—Worship, community, and Scripture all echo heaven's voice.
4. *Refuse Comparison*—Your identity is not measured against others; it is rooted in Christ.

5. *Anchor in Scripture*—Meditate on verses that affirm who you are.

## SCRIPTURES THAT AFFIRM IDENTITY

- "Therefore, if anyone is in Christ, the new creation has come: The old has gone, the new is here! " (2 Corinthians 5:17).
- "For you are all children of God through faith in Christ Jesus" (Galatians 3:26).
- "You are the light of the world. A town built on a hill cannot be hidden" (Matthew 5:14).
- "You are God's workmanship, created in Christ Jesus to do good works" (Ephesians 2:10).

## PRAYER

Father, remind me daily that my identity is found in You, not in the opinions of others. Remove the false labels I have carried and replace them with Your eternal truth. Help me live as Your chosen, beloved, and redeemed child. Amen.

## DISCUSSION & REFLECTION

1. What false labels has God removed from your life?

_____

_____

_____

_____

_____

2. Which Scriptures most strongly affirm your true identity in Christ?

_____

_____

_____

_____

_____

3. How can you remind yourself daily that your worth is received, not earned?

_____

_____

_____

_____

_____

_____

4. Where do you need to start living from identity instead of striving for it?

_____

_____

_____

_____

_____

_____

# CHAPTER 7
# GOD'S CONVERSATION ABOUT YOUR PURPOSE

> Before I formed you in the womb I knew you, before you
> were born I set you apart; I appointed you as a prophet
> to the nations.

JEREMIAH 1:5

So many people spend their lives asking, "Why am I here? "
The world offers countless answers—career, success, relationships, possessions. But true purpose does not begin with self;
it begins with God.

Jeremiah 1:5 reveals that before you took your first breath, God
had already written purpose into your design. You are not an accident.
You are not random. You are intentional. Heaven had a plan for you
long before earth knew your name.

Ephesians 2:10 reinforces this: "For we are God's workmanship,
created in Christ Jesus to do good works, which God prepared in
advance for us to do." You are God's masterpiece, handcrafted with
gifts, passions, and opportunities that align with His eternal plan.

## YOU WERE MADE ON PURPOSE

When God created you, He did not mass-produce a copy. He formed you uniquely, with specific strengths, experiences, and desires. Even your struggles and scars are woven into your calling.

Psalm 139:16 says, "All the days ordained for me were written in Your book before one of them came to be." This means your purpose is not an afterthought; it is embedded in God's eternal conversation about you.

## CASE STUDY: JEREMIAH'S CALLING

Jeremiah wrestled with insecurity. When God declared his calling, Jeremiah replied, "I do not know how to speak; I am too young" (Jeremiah 1:6). But God silenced his excuses: "Do not say, 'I am too young.' You must go to everyone I send you to and say whatever I command you" (v. 7).

Purpose is not about your ability; it is about God's assignment. Where you feel unqualified, God's power qualifies you.

## CASE STUDY: ESTHER'S ASSIGNMENT

Esther's rise to queenship looked like coincidence, but Mordecai recognized divine purpose: "Who knows but that you have come to your royal position for such a time as this?" (Esther 4:14).

Her courage to step into that purpose saved a nation. Esther's story reminds us that purpose is often bigger than personal comfort—it is about impact on others.

## CASE STUDY: PAUL'S MISSION

Paul declared in Galatians 1:15–16: "But when God, who set me apart from my mother's womb and called me by His grace, was pleased to reveal His Son in me so that I might preach Him among the Gentiles…"

Even Paul's past as a persecutor was redeemed into his calling. Your mistakes do not erase God's purpose—they can become the very backdrop for His glory.

## DISCOVERING PURPOSE THROUGH GIFTS AND PASSIONS

God often plants clues to your purpose in the form of passions and gifts. What stirs your heart? What burdens will not let you go? What talents flow naturally from you?

Romans 12:6 says, "We have different gifts, according to the grace given to each of us." Your unique blend of grace and gifting points toward the good works God prepared for you.

## PURPOSE IN EVERY SEASON

Purpose is not limited to one grand assignment; it unfolds through seasons.

- For Moses, purpose began in Pharaoh's palace, shifted to the wilderness, and culminated at the Red Sea.
- For Ruth, purpose unfolded through loyalty in hardship, leading her into the lineage of Christ.
- For you, each stage—childhood, work, family, ministry— carries pieces of your larger calling.

Even in hidden or waiting seasons, God is shaping you for the next step of purpose.

## OBSTACLES TO LIVING IN PURPOSE

1. *Comparison*—Looking at others can make you devalue your own calling.
2. *Fear*—Like Jeremiah, we often feel unqualified.

3. *Distraction*—The busyness of life can drown out God's voice.
4. *Doubt*—Questioning whether you really heard God can stall your obedience.

But remember: the enemy cannot steal your purpose—he can only try to convince you not to walk in it.

## ALIGNING DAILY CHOICES WITH PURPOSE

Purpose is not only about big decisions, it is about daily alignment. Every choice either moves you closer to or further from your calling.

- Choosing prayer over distraction sharpens your hearing.
- Choosing obedience over hesitation strengthens your faith.
- Choosing service over selfishness reflects Christ's heart.

When your small steps align with God's eternal conversation, your larger purpose unfolds naturally.

## PRACTICAL STEPS TO WALK IN PURPOSE

1. *Seek God in Prayer*—Ask, "Lord, reveal my purpose."
2. *Study Scripture*—God's Word confirms identity and calling.
3. *Examine Your Passions*—Notice what burdens or excites your heart.
4. *Listen for Opportunities*—Purpose often reveals itself in open doors.
5. *Take Small Steps*—Purpose grows clearer as you walk it out.

## PURPOSE IS ALWAYS ABOUT JESUS

Ultimately, all callings point back to Christ. Whether your purpose plays out in ministry, business, family, or art, the goal is the same: to glorify Jesus. Colossians 3:17 says, "And whatever you do, whether in word or deed, do it all in the name of the Lord Jesus."

Your purpose is not self-fulfillment; it is God-glorification.

## PRAYER

Lord, reveal my purpose and give me courage to walk in it. Help me to see beyond fear, comparison, and doubt. Teach me to align my daily choices with the works You have prepared in advance. May my life declare Your glory in every season. Amen.

## DISCUSSION & REFLECTION

1. What passions and gifts reveal your calling?

_____

_____

_____

_____

_____

_____

2. How have past struggles or scars shaped your purpose?

_____

_____

_____

_____

_____

3. What daily choices can you align more closely with God's calling?

_____

_____

_____

_____

_____

4. Where is God inviting you to step out in courage, like Jeremiah or Esther?

_____

_____

_____

_____

_____

# CHAPTER 8
# GOD'S CONVERSATION ABOUT YOUR FUTURE

> For I know the plans I have for you,' declares the Lord, 'plans to prosper you and not to harm you, plans to give you hope and a future.'
>
> JEREMIAH 29:11

When uncertainty fills the air and the future feels cloudy, many wonder: *What's next? Will I be okay? Does God even see what's ahead?* The Bible assures us that heaven is not silent about tomorrow. God Himself has spoken: your future is in His hands, and His plans are good.

Jeremiah 29:11 is not a vague encouragement; it is a divine declaration. God does not simply wish you well. He has designed your future with hope woven into its fabric.

## YOUR FUTURE IS SECURE IN THE PLANNER

It is natural to want details. We want God to hand us a map, step by step, year by year. But God often does not reveal the plan—He reveals Himself.

Your future is not secure because you know every twist and turn ahead. Your future is secure because you know the One guiding you. Proverbs 3:5–6 says: "Trust in the Lord with all your heart and lean not on your own understanding; in all your ways submit to Him, and He will make your paths straight."

Faith is not about having clarity. It is about having confidence in the Planner.

## CASE STUDY: ABRAHAM'S JOURNEY

When God called Abraham, He did not give him a full itinerary. He simply said, "Go from your country, your people, and your father's household to the land I will show you" (Genesis 12:1).

Abraham stepped out without knowing the destination, because he trusted the One leading. His obedience birthed a future bigger than he could imagine—a nation, a covenant, a legacy of faith. Your future unfolds the same way: one step of obedience at a time.

## CASE STUDY: JOSEPH'S DREAMS

Joseph's future was revealed through dreams of leadership, but the path looked nothing like the promise. Betrayal, slavery, and prison all seemed to contradict his destiny. Yet each step was preparing him for the palace.

Genesis 50:20 captures the truth: "You intended to harm me, but God intended it for good to accomplish what is now being done, the saving of many lives." Your future is not ruined by detours. What the enemy means for harm, God weaves into purpose.

## CASE STUDY: THE EARLY CHURCH

When Jesus ascended, the disciples faced an uncertain future. But He assured them, "You will receive power when the Holy Spirit comes on you" (Acts 1:8). That promise carried them through persecution, opposition, and growth beyond imagination.

God may not tell you all the details, but He promises His presence, His power, and His provision. That is enough for tomorrow.

## LIVING WITH A HOPE-FILLED PERSPECTIVE

Hope is not wishful thinking—it is confident expectation in God's promises. Romans 15:13 says: "May the God of hope fill you with all joy and peace as you trust in Him, so that you may overflow with hope by the power of the Holy Spirit."

To live hope-filled is to wake up each day expecting God to be faithful, even when circumstances look bleak. Hope lifts your eyes from fear of the unknown to confidence in the Unchanging One.

## THE ENEMY'S LIE VS. GOD'S TRUTH

**The lie:** *Your future is uncertain, fragile, or ruined.*
**The truth:** *Your future is written in God's book* (Psalm 139:16).

**The lie:** *You've missed your chance.*
**The truth:** *God redeems lost time* (Joel 2:25).

**The lie:** *Tomorrow holds only anxiety.*
**The truth:** *God's mercies are new every morning* (Lamentations 3:22–23).

Every fear about the future can be countered with a promise from God's eternal conversation.

## PRACTICAL WAYS TO TRUST GOD WITH YOUR FUTURE

1. *Pray Daily Surrender*—Begin each day with, "Lord, my times are in Your hands."
2. *Hold Plans Loosely*—James 4:15 reminds us to say, "If it is the Lord's will, we will live and do this or that."

3. *Focus on Today's Step*—Jesus said, "Do not worry about tomorrow" (Matthew 6:34). Faith walks one day at a time.
4. *Anchor in Scripture*—Keep promises like Jeremiah 29:11 close when anxiety rises.
5. *Testify to His Faithfulness*—Remember how God carried you before; it is proof He will carry you again.

## ILLUSTRATION: THE GPS GUIDE

Think of your journey like driving with GPS. You do not see the whole map—you only see the next turn. But you trust the voice guiding you. If you take a wrong turn, the GPS recalculates and gets you back on track.

The Holy Spirit works the same way. He does not overwhelm you with the full picture. He simply says, "This is the way; walk in it" (Isaiah 30:21).

## PRAYER

God, thank You that my future is in Your hands. When I cannot see the way, remind me that You are the Planner, and Your plans are good. Fill me with hope, strengthen my faith, and teach me to walk each step with trust. Amen.

## DISCUSSION & REFLECTION

1. How has God reassured you in uncertain times?

_____

_____

_____

_____

_____

2. What promises from Scripture anchor you when the future feels unclear?

_____

_____

_____

_____

_____

_____

3. What does it mean to live with a hope-filled perspective in your daily life?

_____

_____

_____

_____

_____

_____

4. Where do you need to surrender your plans to God's hands?

_____

_____

_____

_____

_____

_____

# CHAPTER 9
# GOD'S CONVERSATION ABOUT YOUR TRIALS

> Consider it pure joy, my brothers and sisters, whenever you face trials of many kinds, because you know that the testing of your faith produces perseverance. Let perseverance finish its work so that you may be mature and complete, not lacking anything.
>
> JAMES 1:2–4

It is easy to assume that hardship means God has forgotten us. But Scripture reminds us that trials are not proof of abandonment—they are evidence that God is refining, strengthening, and preparing us.

James 1:2–4 tells us to "consider it pure joy" when we face trials. Not because the trial itself is enjoyable, but because of what it produces—perseverance, maturity, and completeness. God uses pressure to reveal purity and storms to strengthen roots.

When you face a trial, heaven is not silent. God is speaking over you: *"This will not destroy you. This will develop you."*

## CASE STUDY: JOSEPH'S TRIAL

Joseph's life illustrates how trials position us for destiny. Betrayed by his brothers, sold into slavery, and unjustly imprisoned, Joseph could have concluded that God had abandoned him.

But years later, standing as governor of Egypt, he declared to his brothers: "You intended to harm me, but God intended it for good to accomplish what is now being done, the saving of many lives" (Genesis 50:20).

The very pit that humiliated Joseph positioned him for a palace that would save nations. Your trial may look like a setback, but heaven calls it a setup.

## CASE STUDY: JOB'S PERSEVERANCE

Few people faced trials like Job. He lost his wealth, his children, and his health. Yet in the midst of devastation, Job declared: "Though He slay me, yet will I hope in Him" (Job 13:15).

At the end of his trial, Job testified:

"My ears had heard of You, but now my eyes have seen You" (Job 42:5). Trials move us from knowing about God to knowing God personally.

## CASE STUDY: PAUL'S THORN

Paul, despite his powerful ministry, described a "thorn in the flesh" that he pleaded with God to remove. Yet God responded: "My grace is sufficient for you, for My power is made perfect in weakness" (2 Corinthians 12:9).

Paul's trial taught him that weakness is not a barrier; it is a platform for God's strength.

## THE PURPOSE OF TRIALS

Trials are purposeful, not random. Scripture reveals several reasons God allows them:

1. *To Test Faith*—Trials reveal whether we trust circumstances or Christ.
2. *To Build Character*—Romans 5:3–4: "Suffering produces perseverance; perseverance, character; and character, hope."
3. *To Produce Endurance*—Like muscles strengthened by resistance, faith grows under pressure.
4. *To Display God's Glory*—In John 9, a man born blind was healed so that "the works of God might be displayed in him."

## ILLUSTRATION: THE REFINING FIRE

Gold is purified by fire. The heat separates impurities so that the metal becomes more valuable and radiant. In the same way, trials refine believers.

Peter said: "These have come so that the proven genuineness of your faith—of greater worth than gold…may result in praise, glory, and honor when Jesus Christ is revealed" (1 Peter 1:7). Your trial is not evidence of rejection—it is evidence of refinement.

## ENCOURAGEMENT IN THE MIDST OF TRIALS

When you walk through storms, remember:

- You are not alone. God promised, "When you pass through the waters, I will be with you" (Isaiah 43:2).
- You are not defeated. "No weapon forged against you will prevail" (Isaiah 54:17).
- You are not forgotten. God has engraved you on the palms of His hands (Isaiah 49:16).

## TRIALS AS TESTIMONIES

Your trials are not wasted—they become testimonies that encourage others. Paul wrote in 2 Corinthians 1:4: "[God] comforts us in all our troubles, so that we can comfort those in any trouble with the comfort we ourselves receive from God." What you endure becomes a source of strength for someone else.

## PRACTICAL WAYS TO ENDURE TRIALS

1. *Stay Anchored in Scripture*—Declare God's promises over your pain.
2. *Pray Honestly*—God can handle your questions and tears.
3. *Lean on Community*—Do not walk alone; let others carry you in prayer.
4. *Look for Growth*—Ask, "Lord, what are You teaching me here? "
5. *Keep Eternity in View*—Trials are temporary; glory is eternal (2 Corinthians 4:17).

## PRAYER

Lord, give me strength in my trials, and let my life testify of Your faithfulness. When I am tempted to despair, remind me that You are refining me, not abandoning me. Turn my trials into testimonies that point others to Your glory. Amen.

## DISCUSSION & REFLECTION

1. How have trials in your past deepened your faith?

_____

_____

_____

_____

_____

_____

2. Which Scriptures have anchored you during hardship?

_____

_____

_____

_____

_____

_____

3. How can your current or past trial be used to encourage someone else?

_____

_____

_____

_____

_____

_____

4. In what ways can you shift your perspective from pain to purpose?

_____

_____

_____

_____

_____

_____

# CHAPTER 10
# GOD'S CONVERSATION ABOUT YOUR RELATIONSHIPS

> By this everyone will know that you are My disciples, if you love one another.
>
> JOHN 13:35

God never designed us to live in isolation. From the beginning, He declared, "It is not good for man to be alone" (Genesis 2:18). Relationships—family, friendships, community, and even difficult connections—are part of God's plan to reflect His heart.

At the center of that reflection is love. Jesus said love is the ultimate mark of discipleship. The strength of our relationships is not measured by convenience but by the willingness to love as He has loved us.

## LOVE AT THE CORE

The foundation of every godly relationship is love—unconditional, sacrificial, and enduring. Paul described it in 1 Corinthians 13:

- Love is patient and kind.
- Love is not proud or self-seeking.
- Love keeps no record of wrongs.
- Love never fails.

This is not sentiment; it is commitment. Love is God's language, and when we love others, we echo heaven's conversation on earth.

## FORGIVENESS: THE KEY TO HEALING

Relationships inevitably encounter conflict. People hurt, disappoint, and betray. But forgiveness is God's way of keeping relationships from collapsing under the weight of offense.

Jesus taught us to pray, "Forgive us our debts, as we also have forgiven our debtors" (Matthew 6:12). Forgiveness is not optional—it is essential.

Forgiveness does not mean excusing wrong or forgetting pain. It means releasing others into God's hands, freeing ourselves from bitterness, and making room for reconciliation.

## RECONCILIATION: GOD'S AGENDA

2 Corinthians 5:18–19 declares: "All this is from God, who reconciled us to Himself through Christ and gave us the ministry of reconciliation."

If God reconciled us through Jesus, then we are called to be reconcilers. Our relationships are meant to showcase God's power to bring peace where division once ruled.

## CASE STUDY: JOSEPH AND HIS BROTHERS

Joseph's story is not just about trials and destiny—it is also about relationships. After years of betrayal and separation, Joseph forgave his brothers and provided for them during famine.

He could have sought revenge, but instead he declared, "You

intended to harm me, but God intended it for good" (Genesis 50:20). Forgiveness transformed a fractured family into a reconciled one.

## CASE STUDY: THE PRODIGAL SON

In Luke 15, Jesus told of a father whose son wasted his inheritance and returned in shame. Instead of rejection, the father ran to embrace him.

This parable is not only about God's love for us—it is also a model for how relationships can be restored. Grace runs faster than shame.

## CASE STUDY: PAUL AND BARNABAS

Paul and Barnabas once disagreed so sharply that they parted ways (Acts 15:36–40). Yet later, Paul spoke warmly of Barnabas and even requested John Mark—whom the disagreement was about—to join him in ministry (2 Timothy 4:11).

This shows that even broken relationships can find new life when forgiveness and humility prevail.

## THE COST OF LOVE

Loving others is not always easy. It requires:

- Patience when others grow slowly.
- Humility when we want to be right.
- Sacrifice when it costs us time and comfort.
- Grace when we are tempted to hold grudges.

Jesus demonstrated this kind of love by laying down His life. He calls us to do the same in our relationships—not necessarily through death, but through daily selflessness.

## PRACTICAL WAYS TO STRENGTHEN RELATIONSHIPS

1. *Listen Well*—Give others the gift of attention.
2. *Speak Life*—Use words that build up, not tear down.
3. *Resolve Quickly*—Do not let offense linger; seek reconciliation early.
4. *Serve Faithfully*—Relationships thrive when we put others first.
5. *Pray Consistently*—Lift up your family, friends, and even enemies before God.

## ILLUSTRATION: THE BRIDGE BUILDER

Picture two cliffs separated by a deep chasm. On one side stands you, and on the other stands someone you have been estranged from. Love is the bridge, forgiveness is the foundation, and reconciliation is the crossing.

God calls us not to stare across the divide but to begin building bridges that reflect His reconciling heart.

## PRAYER

Father, help me to love others as You have loved me. Heal broken places in my relationships and make me an agent of reconciliation. Teach me to forgive as I have been forgiven and to extend grace that reflects Your heart. Amen.

## DISCUSSION & REFLECTION

1. How has God spoken to you personally about forgiveness?

_____

_____

_____

_____

_____

_____

2. What relationships in your life need fresh love and attention?

_____

_____

_____

_____

_____

_____

3. Where is God calling you to build bridges of reconciliation?

_____

_____

_____

_____

_____

_____

4. How can you embody Christ's love in practical, daily ways?

_____

_____

_____

_____

_____

_____

_____

# CHAPTER 11
# GOD'S CONVERSATION ABOUT YOUR DESTINY

> For those God foreknew He also predestined to be
> conformed to the image of His Son, that He might be
> the firstborn among many brothers and sisters.

ROMANS 8:29

W hen people think of destiny, they often picture a place, a position, or a personal achievement. But Scripture defines destiny differently. According to Romans 8:29, destiny is not merely where you go but who you become.

Your destiny is to be shaped into the likeness of Jesus Christ. Every event, every season, every blessing, and every trial works toward this eternal purpose. God is less concerned with the titles you carry than with the transformation you undergo.

## DESTINY IS SECURE IN CHRIST

Because destiny is anchored in Christ, it cannot be stolen by circumstances or derailed by human failure. Romans 8:30 continues:

"And those He predestined, He also called; those He called, He also justified; those He justified, He also glorified."

Notice the certainty—what God begins, He completes. Your destiny is secure because it is tied to His eternal plan, not your fragile ability. Philippians 1:6 reassures us: "He who began a good work in you will carry it on to completion until the day of Christ Jesus."

## CASE STUDY: JOSEPH'S DESTINY

Joseph's journey to destiny was not straightforward. Dreams of leadership were followed by betrayal, slavery, and prison. Yet at the end, Joseph declared: "You intended to harm me, but God intended it for good to accomplish what is now being done, the saving of many lives" (Genesis 50:20).

Joseph's destiny was not about sitting in Pharaoh's palace—it was about becoming a man who could steward power with integrity and save nations with wisdom. Destiny shapes who you are before it positions where you are.

## CASE STUDY: MOSES' DESTINY

Moses' destiny was not simply leading Israel out of Egypt. It was becoming a friend of God (Exodus 33:11). The burning bush, the plagues, the Red Sea—all of it shaped Moses into a leader who carried God's presence.

Your destiny, too, is more about intimacy than activity—more about knowing God than performing for Him.

## CASE STUDY: PETER'S DESTINY

Peter's destiny was not just about preaching at Pentecost; it was about transformation. From an impulsive fisherman who denied Jesus three times, he became the bold apostle who declared Christ before thousands.

His destiny was fulfilled not when he achieved greatness but when Christ's likeness was formed in his weakness.

## DESTINY AS TRANSFORMATION

Romans 12:2 says: "Do not conform to the pattern of this world, but be transformed by the renewing of your mind."

Destiny is not external success—it is internal transformation. The Spirit reshapes our thinking, renews our hearts, and conforms us daily to Christ. This means every small act of obedience, every moment of surrender, and every response of faith is shaping destiny in you.

## DESTINY IS BIGGER THAN YOU

God's conversation about your destiny is not only personal—it is generational. Joseph saved nations. Esther preserved her people. Paul carried the gospel to the Gentiles.

Your destiny will ripple beyond your lifetime. What God does in you today becomes legacy for tomorrow.

## OBSTACLES TO DESTINY

1. *Comparison*—Looking at others' journeys blinds you to your own calling.
2. *Impatience*—Destiny unfolds in God's timing, not ours.
3. *Fear*—The enemy uses fear to make you shrink back from bold steps.
4. *Misunderstanding*—Believing destiny is about success, not Christlikeness.

But God reminds us: "The one who calls you is faithful, and He will do it" (1 Thessalonians 5:24).

## DAILY CHOICES THAT SHAPE DESTINY

Destiny is not fulfilled in one dramatic moment—it is formed in daily decisions:

- Choosing prayer over distraction.
- Choosing holiness over compromise.
- Choosing service over self.
- Choosing faith over fear.
- Choosing obedience when it costs.

Every choice either conforms you more to Christ or distracts you from Him.

## ILLUSTRATION: THE SCULPTOR'S CHISEL

Think of a sculptor working on marble. Every strike of the chisel seems harsh, but each one reveals beauty hidden inside.

God is the Master Sculptor. Every season, whether joyous or painful, is a strike of His chisel, shaping you into Christ's likeness. Destiny is not when the marble remains untouched but when it becomes a masterpiece reflecting His image.

## LIVING WITH DESTINY IN MIND

To live with destiny in mind is to measure life not by comfort but by conformity to Christ. It is to ask daily, "Am I looking more like Jesus?"

Colossians 3:4 reminds us: "When Christ, who is your life, appears, then you also will appear with Him in glory." That is destiny fulfilled—standing before Him, complete in His likeness.

## PRAYER

Jesus, shape me into Your likeness and fulfill Your destiny through me. Remove every distraction that pulls me away from Your purpose. Help me to live each day with eternity in view, knowing that my future is secure in You. Amen.

## DISCUSSION & REFLECTION

1. What does living with destiny in mind look like for you personally?

_____

_____

_____

_____

_____

_____

2. What daily choices help you grow into Christ's image?

_____

_____

_____

_____

_____

_____

3. How does seeing destiny as transformation, not just destination, shift your perspective?

_____

_____

_____

_____

_____

_____

4. Where do you see God's chisel shaping you right now?

_____

_____

_____

_____

_____

_____

## CHAPTER 12
# GOD'S CONVERSATION ABOUT YOUR WORK

> Whatever you do, work at it with all your heart, as working for the Lord, not for human masters.

COLOSSIANS 3:23

W ork is often reduced to survival—a paycheck, a duty, a grind. But God sees your work differently. In His eternal conversation, work is not just activity—it is worship. When you labor with integrity, faithfulness, and excellence, your work becomes an offering to Him.

Colossians 3:23 reframes work as sacred. Whether you are in a corporate office, a classroom, a factory, a kitchen, or serving at home, your labor can glorify God. Worship is not limited to Sunday songs; it includes Monday assignments, Tuesday deadlines, and every act done unto the Lord.

## GOD'S DESIGN FOR WORK

From the very beginning, God designed work as part of human purpose. In Genesis 2:15, before sin entered the world, God placed

Adam in the garden "to work it and take care of it." Work was never meant to be punishment—it was participation in God's creation.

Sin corrupted work with frustration, sweat, and struggle (Genesis 3:17–19), but Christ redeems work by restoring its meaning. Now, in Christ, every task becomes an act of worship that reflects God's kingdom on earth.

## WORK THAT REFLECTS GOD'S KINGDOM

When you show up with honesty, diligence, and kindness, your workplace becomes a stage for God's glory. Jesus said in Matthew 5:16: "Let your light shine before others, that they may see your good deeds and glorify your Father in heaven."

Your work ethic, your words, your character—they preach louder than sermons in many settings. Work is evangelism in action.

## CASE STUDY: DANIEL IN BABYLON

Daniel was taken as an exile to Babylon, placed in government service under pagan kings. Yet Scripture says: "Daniel so distinguished himself by his exceptional qualities that the king planned to set him over the whole kingdom" (Daniel 6:3).

Daniel's integrity and excellence pointed to the God he served. Even when threatened with death, Daniel's commitment never wavered. His work was his witness.

## CASE STUDY: PAUL AS A TENTMAKER

Though Paul was an apostle, he also worked with his hands as a tentmaker (Acts 18:3). His labor provided for his needs and demonstrated that ministry is not confined to pulpits. Paul modeled that all work, when done for God, is sacred.

## EXCELLENCE AS WORSHIP

Excellence in work is not about perfection—it is about wholehearted-ness. Colossians 3:23 says, "with all your heart." That means giving your best, not just when people are watching, but because God is always watching.

Excellence honors God, serves people, and testifies of the king-dom. Sloppiness, laziness, or dishonesty misrepresents God's charac-ter. But diligence, creativity, and integrity display His nature.

## WORK AND CALLING

Ephesians 2:10 says you are created for "good works prepared in advance." This does not only mean ministry assignments; it includes daily labor. Your vocation—whether teaching, building, healing, managing, or serving—is part of God's calling.

Calling is not divided into "sacred" and "secular." Every sphere of work is sacred when surrendered to God. A nurse's care, a teacher's lesson, a carpenter's project, a leader's decisions—all become acts of worship when done in Christ's name.

## CHALLENGES IN WORK

Work can be draining, unfair, or undervalued. Bosses may be harsh, systems unjust, or efforts overlooked. Yet Colossians 3:24 reminds us: "It is the Lord Christ you are serving."

When you remember that your ultimate boss is Christ, your perspective shifts. You work not for applause but for eternal reward.

## PRACTICAL WAYS TO HONOR GOD IN WORK

1. *Start with Prayer*—Dedicate each day's tasks to the Lord.
2. *Work with Integrity*—Refuse shortcuts or dishonesty.
3. *Serve with Joy*—Let your attitude reflect Christ's peace.

4. *Pursue Excellence*—Do your best even in small assignments.
5. *Be a Witness*—Use kindness and patience as testimonies.

## ILLUSTRATION: THE CRAFTSMAN'S SIGNATURE

Skilled craftsmen often sign their work, not for fame but as a mark of ownership and pride. In the same way, when you work with excellence, you are signing your labor with God's name. Every completed task whispers, "This reflects my Father's character."

## WORK AND REST

While God calls us to diligence, He also calls us to rest. Sabbath reminds us that our identity is not in productivity but in being His. Work finds balance when paired with rest that honors Him.

## PRAYER

Lord, help me to honor You in my work. Teach me to see my vocation not as a burden but as a place of worship. Let my labor reflect Your kingdom through integrity, diligence, and love. May everything I do glorify You. Amen.

## DISCUSSION & REFLECTION

1. How can you view your work as part of God's calling?

_____

_____

_____

_____

_____

_____

2. What does excellence in your work look like in this season?

_____

_____

_____

_____

_____

_____

3. Where do you need to shift from working for people's approval to working for God's glory?

_____

_____

_____

_____

_____

_____

4. How might your workplace become a stage for God's presence?

_____

_____

_____

_____

_____

_____

# CHAPTER 13
# GOD'S CONVERSATION ABOUT YOUR FINANCES

> The earth is the Lord's, and everything in it, the world, and all who live in it.
>
> PSALM 24:1

O ne of the most freeing truths about money is this: you do not own it. Psalm 24:1 reminds us that the earth, and everything in it, belongs to the Lord. That includes the resources in your account, the possessions in your home, and the opportunities you steward.

We are not owners—we are stewards. Ownership breeds pride and anxiety. Stewardship breeds humility and responsibility. When you recognize that your finances belong to God, every dollar becomes a tool, not just for your benefit but for His purposes.

## FINANCES AS A KINGDOM TOOL

Finances are not evil. Money itself is neutral—it simply reflects the values of the one who manages it. Scripture says in 1 Timothy 6:10:

"The love of money is a root of all kinds of evil." The problem is not money, but misplaced affection.

In God's hands, money becomes a tool to bless others, meet needs, advance the gospel, and reflect heaven's generosity on earth.

2 Corinthians 9:6–8 captures this beautifully: "Whoever sows sparingly will also reap sparingly, and whoever sows generously will also reap generously. Each of you should give what you have decided in your heart to give, not reluctantly or under compulsion, for God loves a cheerful giver. And God is able to bless you abundantly, so that in all things at all times, having all that you need, you will abound in every good work."

Generosity is not subtraction; it is multiplication in God's economy.

## CASE STUDY: THE WIDOW'S OFFERING

In Mark 12:41–44, Jesus observed people giving at the temple. Many gave large amounts, but one widow gave two small coins. Jesus declared that she had given more than all the rest, because she gave out of poverty with full trust in God.

This shows us that heaven measures giving not by size but by sacrifice. God's conversation about finances is less about numbers and more about the heart behind them.

## CASE STUDY: THE MACEDONIAN CHURCHES

Paul describes the Macedonian believers in 2 Corinthians 8:2–3: "In the midst of a very severe trial, their overflowing joy and their extreme poverty welled up in rich generosity. For I testify that they gave as much as they were able, and even beyond their ability."

Even in lack, they chose generosity. Their giving was a testimony that resources may be limited, but God's provision is unlimited.

## CASE STUDY: THE EARLY CHURCH

In Acts 4:32–35, the early believers shared their possessions so that "there were no needy persons among them." They did not cling to ownership—they lived as stewards. This radical generosity displayed heaven's culture on earth and fueled the spread of the gospel.

## GENEROSITY REFLECTS GOD'S HEART

God is the ultimate giver: "For God so loved the world that He gave His one and only Son" (John 3:16). When we give, we mirror His character.

Generosity demonstrates trust. It says, "I believe God is my source, not my bank account." It shifts our focus from scarcity to abundance, from fear to faith.

## OBSTACLES TO STEWARDSHIP

1. *Fear of Lack*—Worrying there will not be enough hinders generosity.
2. *Materialism*—Believing identity is tied to possessions.
3. *Selfishness*—Using resources only for personal gain.
4. *Mismanagement*—Poor stewardship leads to unnecessary struggle.

But Jesus reminds us: "Seek first His kingdom and His righteousness, and all these things will be given to you as well" (Matthew 6:33).

## PRACTICAL PRINCIPLES FOR STEWARDSHIP

1. *Acknowledge Ownership*—Start by declaring, "God, this belongs to You."
2. *Give First*—Practice tithing and generosity before spending.
3. *Save Wisely*—Stewardship includes planning for the future.

4. *Live Within Means*—Avoid debt that enslaves (Proverbs 22:7).
5. *Invest in Eternity*—Use resources for kingdom impact, not just temporary comfort.

## ILLUSTRATION: THE OPEN HAND

Picture holding sand in your fist. The tighter you squeeze, the more slips through your fingers. But if you open your hand, you can both hold and receive more. That is how finances work in God's kingdom. Closed fists lose; open hands receive and give freely.

## FINANCES AS WORSHIP

Ultimately, stewardship is worship. Every time you budget with integrity, give with joy, or meet a need with generosity, you are declaring: "God, You are my provider."

Romans 12:1 calls us to offer our whole lives as living sacrifices. That includes our bank accounts.

## PRAYER

God, help me to steward my finances with wisdom and generosity. Teach me to see resources not as mine but as Yours. Deliver me from fear and greed, and make me a cheerful giver who reflects Your heart. Amen.

## DISCUSSION & REFLECTION

1. How does generosity reflect God's heart more than accumulation?

_____
_____
_____
_____
_____
_____

2. Where can you grow in stewardship this season—giving, saving, managing, or trusting?

_____
_____
_____
_____
_____
_____

3. How can your finances advance God's purposes in practical ways?

_____
_____
_____
_____
_____
_____

4. What fears about money do you need to surrender to God's care?

_____
_____
_____
_____
_____
_____

# CHAPTER 14
# GOD'S CONVERSATION ABOUT YOUR HEALING

> Praise the Lord, my soul, and forget not all His benefits
> —who forgives all your sins and heals all your diseases,
> who redeems your life from the pit and crowns you with
> love and compassion, who satisfies your desires with
> good things so that your youth is renewed like the
> eagle's.
>
> PSALM 103:2–5

God's conversation about you includes every part of who you are—body, soul, and spirit. He is not indifferent to your pain, whether physical illness, emotional wounds, or spiritual brokenness. His covenant includes forgiveness and healing. David reminds us not to forget His benefits: He both forgives all your sins and heals all your diseases.

Healing is not a side note in God's Word—it is a reflection of His nature. He revealed Himself as Jehovah Rapha—"The Lord who heals you" (Exodus 15:26). Healing flows out of His identity.

## JESUS THE HEALER

Everywhere Jesus went, He healed. The Gospels record Him opening blind eyes, cleansing lepers, making the lame walk, and raising the dead. Matthew 4:23 summarizes: "Jesus went throughout Galilee, teaching in their synagogues, proclaiming the good news of the kingdom, and healing every disease and sickness among the people."

Healing was not an occasional miracle—it was a central part of His ministry, a demonstration of the kingdom breaking into brokenness.

Hebrews 13:8 assures us: "Jesus Christ is the same yesterday and today and forever." The same Healer who walked the streets of Galilee is still present today.

## INSTANT AND PROCESS HEALING

Sometimes God heals instantly, as with the paralyzed man lowered through the roof (Mark 2:11–12). Other times, healing comes through process. When Jesus healed a blind man in Mark 8:22–25, it happened in stages: first partial sight, then full clarity.

Both instant and progressive healing are valid works of God. What matters most is not the speed of the outcome but the constancy of His presence. Healing may unfold over days, months, or even a lifetime, but the Healer never leaves.

## CASE STUDY: THE WOMAN WITH THE ISSUE OF BLOOD

For twelve years she suffered. Doctors failed her, money was drained, and hope was nearly gone. Yet one touch of Jesus' garment brought complete restoration (Mark 5:25–34).

Her story reminds us that persistence in faith and proximity to Jesus bring breakthrough. Even years of suffering cannot silence God's healing word.

## CASE STUDY: NAAMAN'S CLEANSING

Naaman, a Syrian commander, sought healing from leprosy. Instead of instant drama, God instructed him to dip seven times in the Jordan River (2 Kings 5:10–14). His healing came through obedience to a process.

This illustrates that healing sometimes requires humble steps of faith, even when they do not look spectacular.

## CASE STUDY: PAUL'S THORN

Paul prayed three times for his "thorn in the flesh" to be removed, yet God answered: "My grace is sufficient for you, for My power is made perfect in weakness" (2 Corinthians 12:9).

Not all healing comes in the way we expect. Sometimes God sustains us through weakness to display His strength. Healing is not always the absence of struggle—it is the presence of His sustaining grace.

## THE ROLE OF FAITH AND HOPE

Faith positions us to receive healing, but hope sustains us while we wait. Hebrews 11:1 says: "Now faith is confidence in what we hope for and assurance about what we do not see."

Faith believes God can. Hope trusts God will. And love assures us He is with us, no matter what.

## HEALING FOR THE SOUL

God's healing is not limited to the physical body. Psalm 147:3 declares: "He heals the brokenhearted and binds up their wounds."

Emotional scars, relational wounds, and inner pain matter to Him. Jesus said in Luke 4:18 that He came "to bind up the brokenhearted" and set captives free. Healing includes peace of mind, restoration of joy, and freedom from shame.

## HEALING AS KINGDOM WITNESS

When God heals, it testifies that His kingdom is real. Miracles are signs—pointing beyond themselves to the King. Acts 3 tells of a lame man healed at the temple gate. Peter declared that the miracle was proof of Jesus' resurrection power.

Your healing—whether gradual, immediate, or sustaining grace—becomes a witness of God's faithfulness to those around you.

## PRACTICAL WAYS TO INVITE GOD'S HEALING

1. *Pray Persistently*—Ask, seek, and knock (Matthew 7:7).
2. *Stand on Scripture*—Declare verses like Psalm 103 and Isaiah 53:5.
3. *Seek Community Prayer*—James 5:14–15 encourages calling elders to pray and anoint with oil.
4. *Live in Obedience*—Healing is often connected to walking in God's ways.
5. *Trust God's Timing*—Rest in His sovereignty whether healing is instant or progressive.

## ILLUSTRATION: THE DOCTOR'S PRESENCE

Imagine visiting a skilled doctor. Sometimes he prescribes immediate treatment; other times he schedules a series of therapies. Either way, his presence and care are constant. Likewise, God is not absent in your healing process. His presence is the medicine that sustains you.

## PRAYER

Lord, thank You for being my Healer. Thank You that Your covenant includes forgiveness and wholeness. Strengthen me with hope and faith as I wait for Your work in my body, soul, and spirit. Whether healing comes instantly or through process, remind me that Your presence never leaves. Amen.

## DISCUSSION & REFLECTION

1. How has God touched you with healing—physically, emotionally, or spiritually?

_____

_____

_____

_____

_____

2. Where do you need to invite His healing presence today?

_____

_____

_____

_____

_____

3. How does trusting God's presence through the process shift your perspective?

_____

_____

_____

_____

_____

_____

4. Who around you could be encouraged by your testimony of God's healing grace?

_____

_____

_____

_____

_____

_____

# CHAPTER 15
# GOD'S CONVERSATION ABOUT YOUR LEGACY

> And the things you have heard me say in the presence of many witnesses entrust to reliable people who will also be qualified to teach others.
>
> 2 TIMOTHY 2:2

When people think of legacy, they often imagine what will be said at their funeral or what material possessions they will leave behind. But biblically, legacy is not only about what you leave after you are gone—it is about what you build while you are here.

Legacy is the ripple effect of your faith, your choices, and your investments in others. It is the continuation of God's conversation through your life, echoing into generations you may never meet.

## GOD'S DESIRE FOR GENERATIONAL IMPACT

Throughout Scripture, God speaks not only to individuals but to their descendants. His promises are generational. When He blessed Abraham, He also blessed Isaac and Jacob. When He spoke to David, He promised a lineage that would culminate in Christ.

Psalm 78:4 says: "We will not hide them from their descendants; we will tell the next generation the praiseworthy deeds of the Lord, His power, and the wonders He has done."

God's eternal conversation about you includes how your life testifies to the next generation.

## YOUR WORDS CARRY WEIGHT

Words have the power to shape legacy. Proverbs 18:21 reminds us that "the tongue has the power of life and death."

- When you speak encouragement, you plant seeds of faith.
- When you declare Scripture, you pass on truth that outlives you.
- When you speak forgiveness, you break cycles of bitterness.
- Your legacy is written not only in deeds but in the daily words you sow into others.

## YOUR ACTIONS BUILD FOUNDATIONS

Legacy is also shaped by consistent actions:

- Acts of integrity that model faithfulness.
- Acts of service that inspire others to give.
- Acts of courage that prove faith can endure trial.

Jesus said in Matthew 5:16: "Let your light shine before others, that they may see your good deeds and glorify your Father in heaven." Your actions today become stories tomorrow.

## CASE STUDY: TIMOTHY'S INHERITANCE OF FAITH

Paul reminded Timothy of the faith passed down through his grandmother Lois and mother Eunice (2 Timothy 1:5). Their devotion became his inheritance.

They did not leave Timothy wealth or prestige—they left him faith, the greatest legacy of all.

## CASE STUDY: DAVID'S PREPARATION FOR SOLOMON

David longed to build the temple but was told his son would complete it. Instead of resenting this, David prepared materials, gave instructions, and blessed Solomon (1 Chronicles 22).

David's legacy was not only the victories he won but the foundation he laid for the next generation to succeed.

## CASE STUDY: JESUS AND THE DISCIPLES

Jesus' earthly ministry lasted about three years, yet His legacy continues because He poured into disciples who carried His mission forward. He entrusted truth to them, and they entrusted it to others—fulfilling 2 Timothy 2:2.

Your legacy is multiplied when you invest in people who will pass truth further than you could on your own.

## BUILDING LEGACY NOW

Legacy is not accidental—it is intentional. Every choice today shapes tomorrow's testimony. Ask yourself:

- Am I modeling forgiveness or resentment?
- Am I sowing generosity or selfishness?
- Am I discipling others or only living for myself?

Galatians 6:7 says: "A man reaps what he sows." What you plant now is what the next generation will harvest.

## OBSTACLES TO LEAVING A GODLY LEGACY

1. *Short-Term Thinking*—Living only for today ignores generational impact.
2. *Inconsistency*—Mixed messages confuse those watching your example.
3. *Neglect*—Failing to invest in others leaves the next generation empty-handed.
4. *Bitterness*—Unresolved pain can pass down unhealthy patterns.

God invites you to break cycles and build new legacies rooted in His truth.

## PRACTICAL STEPS TO SHAPE LEGACY

1. *Invest in People*—Pour into children, disciples, and spiritual sons and daughters.
2. *Live With Integrity*—Let your private life match your public witness.
3. *Tell Your Story*—Share testimonies of God's faithfulness.
4. *Give Generously*—Use resources to bless beyond your lifetime.
5. *Pray for Generations*—Pray blessings over children and grandchildren—even spiritual ones.

## ILLUSTRATION: PLANTING TREES YOU WON'T SIT UNDER

Legacy is like planting a tree whose shade you may never enjoy, but future generations will. The fruit and rest they experience will trace back to the seeds you planted.

Your legacy may not be seen fully in your lifetime, but heaven keeps record, and eternity will reveal the harvest.

## PRAYER

Lord, help me to leave a godly legacy that honors You and blesses others. Teach me to sow words, actions, and investments that carry Your truth to generations I may never meet. May my life echo into eternity, pointing always to Jesus. Amen.

## DISCUSSION & REFLECTION

1. What legacy are you currently building through your daily choices?

_____

_____

_____

_____

_____

2. How can you intentionally bless the next generation with your faith and example?

_____

_____

_____

_____

_____

3. Who has passed a spiritual legacy to you, and how can you do the same for others?

_____

_____

_____

_____

_____

_____

4. What seeds can you plant today that will bear fruit long after you are gone?

_____

_____

_____

_____

_____

# PART THREE
# LIVING THE CONVERSATION DAILY

# CHAPTER 16

# SPEAKING WHAT GOD SPEAKS

> The tongue has the power of life and death, and those who love it will eat its fruit.
>
> PROVERBS 18:21

W ords are never neutral. They carry weight, direction, and creative force. With a word, you can build up or tear down, encourage or discourage, release faith, or spread fear. Proverbs 18:21 reminds us that life and death are in the tongue.

This truth flows from God Himself. The very universe was created by His words. Genesis 1 repeats the rhythm: "And God said... and it was so." When God speaks, reality aligns. When we, as His image-bearers, speak, our words also carry impact.

## AGREEING WITH HEAVEN

When we confess God's promises, we align our earthly voice with heaven's eternal conversation. Confession is not merely admitting sin or failure—it is declaring what God has said to be true. Romans 10:9

teaches that salvation itself is activated when we "confess with [our] mouth that Jesus is Lord."

Speaking God's Word reinforces faith. It shifts our perspective, silences the lies of the enemy, and calls unseen realities into being. Hebrews 11:3 explains: "By faith we understand that the universe was formed at God's command, so that what is seen was not made out of what was visible." If creation was framed by God's word, then our lives can be reshaped by declaring His promises.

## CASE STUDY: EZEKIEL IN THE VALLEY OF DRY BONES

In Ezekiel 37, the prophet was led to a valley full of dry bones. God asked, "Can these bones live? "Ezekiel wisely answered, "Sovereign Lord, You alone know." Then God commanded him to prophesy: "Prophesy to these bones and say to them, 'Dry bones, hear the word of the Lord! '" (v. 4).

As Ezekiel spoke, bones rattled, flesh appeared, and breath entered. What was dead came to life through the power of spoken agreement with God. This illustrates a kingdom principle: when you speak what God speaks, lifeless situations receive new life.

## CASE STUDY: JESUS IN THE WILDERNESS

When tempted by Satan in Matthew 4:1–11, Jesus resisted not by silence but by declaring, "It is written." Each temptation was defeated by spoken Scripture.

Notice Jesus didn't merely think the Word. He spoke it. Declaring truth out loud dismantles the enemy's lies and strengthens your faith.

## CASE STUDY: JOSHUA'S CHARGE

In Joshua 1:8, God instructed Joshua: "Keep this Book of the Law always on your lips; meditate on it day and night, so that you may be careful to do everything written in it. Then you will be prosperous and successful."

God didn't only tell Joshua to think about His Word but to keep it on his lips. Speaking the Word was part of his strategy for victory.

## CONFESSION AS DECLARATION

Biblical confession means more than acknowledging sin—it means declaring agreement with God. To "confess" is to "say the same thing."

- When you confess forgiveness, you agree with God that you are cleansed (1 John 1:9).
- When you confess promises, you agree that His Word is true.
- When you confess faith, you declare trust in His nature.

Your tongue becomes a partner in shaping reality according to God's purposes.

## THE CREATIVE FORCE OF WORDS

- Words can create faith (Romans 10:17: "Faith comes by hearing...").
- Words can heal wounds (Proverbs 12:18: "...the tongue of the wise brings healing").
- Words can set direction (James 3:4 compares the tongue to a rudder that steers a ship).
- Words can release blessing (Numbers 6:24–26 records the priestly blessing that spoke peace over Israel).

Every word you speak plants seeds. The question is: will they grow life or death?

## GUARDING YOUR TONGUE

James 3 warns that the tongue, though small, can set a whole forest on fire. Careless words ignite division, but Spirit-led words bring peace.

Psalm 141:3 is a wise prayer: "Set a guard over my mouth, Lord; keep watch over the door of my lips."

Guarding your tongue means choosing silence when tempted to complain, choosing encouragement instead of criticism, and choosing faith-filled declarations over fear-filled words.

## PRACTICAL WAYS TO SPEAK WHAT GOD SPEAKS

1. *Declare Promises Daily*– Speak Scripture aloud over your life.
2. *Bless Others Intentionally*– Use words to affirm and uplift.
3. *Pray the Word*– Turn Bible verses into personal prayers.
4. *Correct Lies Quickly*– When the enemy whispers doubt, respond with truth.
5. *Test Words Before Speaking*– Ask: "Does this agree with God's heart?"

## ILLUSTRATION: THE ECHO CHAMBER

Imagine standing in a canyon. When you shout, your voice echoes back. Speaking God's Word is like releasing His truth into the canyon of your circumstances—the echo you hear back is faith, hope, and alignment with heaven.

## LIVING A LIFESTYLE OF DECLARATION

This is not about empty "positive thinking." It is about grounding your speech in the unshakable truth of Scripture. When you consistently declare what God has said, you train your heart to believe, your mind to renew, and your circumstances to align with His will.

## PRAYER

Lord, help me to guard my tongue and speak words that agree with Your truth. Teach me to declare Your promises daily, to silence lies with Scripture, and to use my words to bring life to others. Amen.

---

## DISCUSSION & REFLECTION

1. What promises of God do you need to begin speaking daily?

_____

_____

_____

_____

_____

2. How can your words bring life to someone else this week?

_____

_____

_____

_____

_____

_____

3. Where have careless words sown discouragement, and how can you replace them with truth?

_____

_____

_____

_____

_____

_____

4. What habits can you create to consistently declare God's Word over your life?

_____

_____

_____

_____

_____

_____

# CHAPTER 17
# WALKING OUT YOUR PROMISES

> We do not want you to become lazy, but to imitate those who through faith and patience inherit what has been promised.
>
> HEBREWS 6:12

F aith is more than mental agreement—it is active trust. Hebrews 11, often called the "Hall of Faith," shows that every hero of faith was remembered not merely for what they believed, but for what they did in response to belief.

- Noah built an ark.
- Abraham left his homeland.
- Moses confronted Pharaoh.
- Rahab hid the spies.

Their actions didn't earn God's promises—they demonstrated trust in them. Faith without works is dead (James 2:17). Living faith walks, moves, obeys.

## PROMISE AND PROCESS

God's promises are sure, but their fulfillment often unfolds through process. Hebrews 6:12 reminds us that promises are inherited "through faith and patience." This combination—trusting God's Word and waiting with endurance—positions us to receive.

- Faith is the confidence.
- Patience is the posture.
- Obedience is the pathway.

## CASE STUDY: ABRAHAM'S STEP OF FAITH

When God called Abraham, He said, "Go from your country, your people and your father's household to the land I will show you" (Genesis 12:1). Abraham had no map, no clarity about the destination—only a promise. Yet he went.

His obedience became the foundation of a covenant that blessed nations. Abraham's faith was not just belief in God's words, but willingness to take steps even when the outcome was unseen.

## CASE STUDY: ISRAEL AND THE PROMISED LAND

God promised Israel a land flowing with milk and honey. Yet they had to march around Jericho, cross the Jordan, and fight battles. The land was given, but they still had to walk into it.

Likewise, God's promises to you are secure, but you must take steps of obedience to possess them.

## CASE STUDY: PETER WALKING ON WATER

When Jesus said, "Come," Peter stepped out of the boat (Matthew 14:29). The miracle happened when his faith moved his feet. The promise of walking on water required participation. Your miracle may be waiting for your movement.

## FAITH AND PATIENCE

We often love the "faith" part but struggle with the "patience" part. Hebrews 10:36 says: "You need to persevere so that when you have done the will of God, you will receive what He has promised."

Patience is not passive waiting—it is active trust that continues in obedience, even when results are delayed. Like a farmer sowing seed, you believe harvest will come in due time (Galatians 6:9).

## OBSTACLES TO WALKING OUT PROMISES

1. *Fear*– The unknown can paralyze obedience.
2. *Doubt*– Questioning whether God really spoke.
3. *Delay*– Waiting seasons can tempt you to quit.
4. *Distraction*– Other voices compete with God's Word.

Overcoming these obstacles requires focus on God's character. His faithfulness is greater than your fear, His Word stronger than your doubt.

## PRACTICAL STEPS TO WALK OUT GOD'S PROMISES

1. Seek God's Word First– Anchor in Scripture, not emotion.
2. Take the Next Step– Obedience is often one step at a time, not the whole journey at once.
3. Stay Consistent– Keep doing what He told you even when progress feels slow.
4. Surround Yourself With Faith– Walk with people who remind you of God's promises.
5. Celebrate Small Wins– Each step is evidence of God's faithfulness.

## ILLUSTRATION: THE BRIDGE OF FAITH

Picture a bridge shrouded in fog. You cannot see the other side, but you know it's there. Every step forward is a choice to trust the structure beneath your feet.

Walking out promises is like crossing that bridge. You don't need to see the destination—you just need to trust the God who built the way.

## FAITH PRODUCES TESTIMONY

When you walk out God's promises, your life becomes a testimony. Others see that faith and patience bring results. Hebrews 11:39 says many of the heroes of faith "were commended for their faith, yet none of them received what had been promised" in full. Still, their obedience changed history.

Your faith journey is not just about your promises—it is about inspiring others to walk in theirs.

## PRAYER

Faithful God, give me strength to walk in obedience to Your promises. Help me to trust You when I cannot see, to keep moving when I feel weary, and to remain patient when fulfillment is delayed. Let my life be a testimony of Your faithfulness. Amen.

## DISCUSSION & REFLECTION

1. What step of obedience is God asking you to take right now?

_____

_____

_____

_____

_____

2. How have you seen faith and patience work together to bring results?

_____

_____

_____

_____

_____

3. Where do fear, doubt, or delay challenge your ability to walk in promises?

_____

_____

_____

_____

_____

_____

4. Who could be encouraged by your testimony of faith in action?

_____

_____

_____

_____

_____

# CHAPTER 18
# SHIFTING ATMOSPHERES THROUGH CONVERSATION

> He got up, rebuked the wind, and said to the waves, 'Quiet! Be still!' Then the wind died down and it was completely calm.
>
> MARK 4:39

Every space you enter carries an atmosphere. It might be filled with peace, tension, joy, or heaviness. What many don't realize is that words often set and shape these unseen environments. Proverbs 18:21 says that life and death are in the tongue. Words are not empty—they carry spirit, tone, and power.

When you speak blessings, encouragement, and truth, you are shifting the spiritual climate. When you speak negativity, fear, or criticism, you reinforce darkness. Your words are not just personal—they are environmental.

## JESUS, THE ATMOSPHERE SHIFTER

In Mark 4, Jesus demonstrated the authority of words over atmosphere. Facing a violent storm, the disciples panicked. Jesus, however, spoke three words: "Quiet! Be still! " Immediately, chaos turned into calm.

This wasn't just about weather; it was about revealing the kingdom. Wherever Jesus went, His words shifted atmospheres:

- To the sick: "Be healed."
- To the dead: "Lazarus, come out!"
- To the sinner: "Your sins are forgiven."
- To the fearful: "Take courage. Do not be afraid."

Every word He spoke carried life, authority, and peace.

## CASE STUDY: PAUL AND SILAS IN PRISON

In Acts 16, Paul and Silas were beaten and chained. Instead of cursing their situation, they prayed and sang hymns. Their words of worship shifted the prison's atmosphere. An earthquake shook the foundations, doors opened, and captives were freed.

Atmosphere is not controlled by location—it is controlled by what you release.

## CASE STUDY: DAVID AND GOLIATH

When David faced Goliath, the giant's words filled Israel's camp with fear. But David's declaration—"The Lord will deliver you into my hands" (1 Samuel 17:46)—shifted the atmosphere from intimidation to faith.

Sometimes the difference between defeat and victory is the declaration you choose to make.

## YOUR AUTHORITY TO SPEAK

As children of God, we carry delegated authority. Matthew 16:19 says: "I will give you the keys of the kingdom of heaven; whatever you bind on earth will be bound in heaven, and whatever you loose on earth will be loosed in heaven."

Your words, when aligned with God's Word, bind chaos and loose peace. They silence lies and release truth. You are not powerless in environments of fear, doubt, or heaviness—you are called to shift them.

## PRACTICAL WAYS TO SHIFT ATMOSPHERES

1. *Speak Peace Into Chaos*– Declare God's shalom over conflict.
2. *Bless, Don't Curse*– Replace criticism with encouragement.
3. *Declare Scripture*– Speak promises that reshape perspectives.
4. *Worship Aloud*– Praise shifts atmospheres like light breaking darkness.
5. *Pray Boldly*– Your prayers release God's will into environments.

## ILLUSTRATION: THERMOSTAT VS. THERMOMETER

A thermometer reflects temperature; a thermostat sets it. Too often, we act like thermometers, mirroring the negativity around us. God calls us to be thermostats—setting spiritual climates through words of faith, hope, and love.

## GUARDING ATMOSPHERE IN YOUR HOME

Your home carries an atmosphere. The words spoken within its walls shape it. Harsh words invite tension; gentle words cultivate peace. Proverbs 15:1 says: "A gentle answer turns away wrath, but a harsh word stirs up anger."

Guard your household by intentionally speaking life. Let Scripture, prayer, and encouragement fill your home with God's presence.

## GUARDING ATMOSPHERE IN YOUR WORKPLACE

Workplaces can be filled with stress and competition. Yet your presence can shift the culture. When you speak calm in crisis, encouragement to coworkers, or truth into confusion, you reflect God's kingdom. Daniel served in a pagan government, but his integrity and words shifted the atmosphere so profoundly that kings sought his counsel.

## THE ENEMY'S COUNTERFEIT

The enemy knows the power of words, which is why he tempts people to gossip, complain, and curse. These darken environments, spread division, and choke faith. But as a believer, you are called to counter darkness with declarations of light.

## LIVING AS AN ATMOSPHERE CARRIER

Shifting atmospheres is not just about moments of prayer—it is a lifestyle. Everywhere you go, your words can carry peace, healing, and faith. Jesus said in Matthew 10:13 that when you enter a home, let your peace rest upon it.

Imagine living so full of God's Word that your very presence changes the climate around you.

## PRAYER

Prince of Peace, let my words shift the atmosphere around me to reflect Your kingdom. Teach me to bless, not curse; to speak peace, not chaos; to declare life, not death. May my mouth release Your authority everywhere I go. Amen.

## DISCUSSION & REFLECTION

1. Where do you need to speak peace into chaos right now?

_____

_____

_____

_____

_____

2. How have your words shifted an atmosphere in the past?

_____

_____

_____

_____

_____

3. What habits can you form to consistently bless and encourage rather than complain?

_____

_____

_____

_____

_____

_____

4. How can you live as a thermostat, not a thermometer, in your daily environments?

_____

_____

_____

_____

_____

# CHAPTER 19
# GENERATIONAL CONVERSATIONS

> Know therefore that the Lord your God is God; He is the
> faithful God, keeping His covenant of love to a thousand
> generations of those who love Him and keep His
> commandments.

DEUTERONOMY 7:9

Unlike human plans, which often focus only on today or tomorrow, God's purposes span generations. When He speaks, He is not only addressing your life but also your children, grandchildren, and descendants yet unborn. His promises are long-term investments, His covenants enduring.

Deuteronomy 7:9 declares that God's faithfulness extends "to a thousand generations." That means the choices you make today and the words you declare now ripple far beyond your lifetime.

## BLESSING THAT OUTLIVES YOU

God designed families to carry His blessing forward. Abraham's obedience didn't just affect him—it shaped Isaac, Jacob, and the nation of

Israel. Psalm 103:17–18 says: "But from everlasting to everlasting the Lord's love is with those who fear Him, and His righteousness with their children's children—with those who keep His covenant and remember to obey His precepts."

Your legacy is not only material—it is spiritual. Your prayers, faith, and obedience can create reservoirs of blessing for generations to drink from.

## BREAKING GENERATIONAL CYCLES

Just as blessings can be passed down, so can broken patterns. Scripture warns of generational cycles of sin, idolatry, or disobedience. But Christ's redemption breaks every chain.

- If your family has carried anger, you can declare peace.
- If your line has known poverty, you can declare provision.
- If cycles of addiction plagued generations before you, you can declare freedom in Christ.

Galatians 3:13 says Christ redeemed us from the curse. That means you have authority to declare truth that breaks destructive patterns and plants new seeds of blessing.

## CASE STUDY: ABRAHAM'S GENERATIONAL COVENANT

When God promised Abraham descendants, He was speaking not just to a man but to a nation. Abraham's faith became the foundation of generational blessing: "All peoples on earth will be blessed through you" (Genesis 12:3). His obedience opened doors for generations he would never meet.

## CASE STUDY: TIMOTHY'S SPIRITUAL INHERITANCE

Paul reminded Timothy of the "sincere faith" that lived first in his grandmother Lois and then his mother Eunice (2 Timothy 1:5). Timothy's strength in ministry was directly connected to the spiritual investments of prior generations. Faith multiplies when passed intentionally.

## CASE STUDY: KING JOSIAH

Josiah inherited a kingdom marked by idolatry. Yet when he discovered the Book of the Law, he broke from generational sin, tore down altars, and restored worship (2 Kings 22–23). His choice redirected a nation's trajectory.

This shows us that even if your generational story includes brokenness, you can be the one to shift the direction.

## SPEAKING BLESSINGS INTO THE FUTURE

Proverbs 18:21 reminds us our words carry life or death. That includes words spoken over our families. You can declare blessings that shape atmospheres for generations:

- "My children will know the Lord."
- "My family will walk in peace and wholeness."
- "We are a household of faith, generosity, and integrity."

Your declarations become seeds. Seeds may not sprout immediately, but in time they produce fruit for future generations.

## PRACTICAL WAYS TO BUILD GENERATIONAL BLESSING

1. *Pray Scripture Over Descendants*– Declare promises like Joshua 24:15: "As for me and my household, we will serve the Lord."
2. *Model Obedience*– Children learn faith by seeing it lived out.
3. *Tell Testimonies*– Share stories of God's faithfulness so they become family memory.

4. *Create Traditions*– Build rhythms of prayer, worship, and generosity that outlast you.
5. *Bless Intentionally*– Speak life over children and grandchildren regularly.

## ILLUSTRATION: PLANTING FOR GENERATIONS

Farmers sometimes plant trees whose fruit they will never eat. Their labor is not for themselves but for future generations. Similarly, when you sow prayer, faith, and obedience, you are planting orchards of blessing for descendants to enjoy.

## ENCOURAGEMENT: YOU CAN BE THE TURNING POINT

Maybe your family history includes cycles of pain, brokenness, or unbelief. The good news: you can be the hinge on which the story turns. In Christ, you have the authority to close doors to curses and open doors to covenant blessing.

Your yes to God today changes the story for those who come after you.

## PRAYER

Lord, let my life and words plant seeds of blessing for generations to come. Break every destructive cycle in my family line, and establish Your truth, peace, and love as the foundation for those who follow. May my obedience echo into generations I will never see. Amen.

## DISCUSSION & REFLECTION

1. What generational patterns in your family need to be broken by God's truth?

_____

_____

_____

_____

_____

2. How can you begin blessing future generations with intentional words and actions?

_____

_____

_____

_____

_____

3. Who in your life is already carrying forward a legacy of faith, and how can you honor that?

_____

_____

_____

_____

_____

4. What seeds can you plant today that will bear fruit long after you're gone?

_____

_____

_____

_____

_____

_____

# CHAPTER 20
# YOUR PLACE IN THE ETERNAL CONVERSATION

> And God raised us up with Christ and seated us with
> Him in the heavenly realms in Christ Jesus.
>
> EPHESIANS 2:6

God's conversation is not distant, exclusive, or reserved for a few. Through Christ, you have been raised and seated in heavenly places. This means you don't simply observe heaven's dialogue—you participate in it.

Ephesians 2:6 is not a future promise but a present reality. Right now, by faith, you are seated with Christ. That seat is a place of privilege, perspective, and partnership. You are not a spectator—you are a participant in the eternal conversation.

## HEAVEN'S ONGOING CONVERSATION

What is this eternal conversation? Revelation 4–5 gives us a glimpse:

- Angels worship around God's throne, declaring, "Holy, holy, holy."

- Elders cast their crowns, proclaiming His worth.
- Saints and creatures in heaven and on earth cry out, "To Him who sits on the throne... be praise and honor and glory and power."

It is a constant chorus of worship, intercession, and declaration. And Scripture says you are included in this heavenly dialogue.

## PRAYER AS PARTICIPATION

When you pray, you are not sending words into empty air—you are joining a conversation already happening in heaven. Romans 8:34 says Jesus is at the right hand of God interceding for us. Hebrews 7:25 adds that He lives to make intercession.

Prayer means partnering with Christ's intercession. Your voice becomes one with His. When you pray according to God's Word, you echo heaven's agenda.

## WORSHIP AS AGREEMENT

Worship is another way we join heaven's chorus. Every time you lift your voice in praise, you are harmonizing with angels and saints around the throne. Psalm 22:3 says God inhabits the praises of His people. Worship shifts perspective, lifts burdens, and reminds you that you belong to something greater than yourself. Worship is not warm-up before a sermon; it is eternal participation in heaven's language.

## DECLARATIONS AS ALIGNMENT

When you declare God's Word, you align your life and atmosphere with His eternal truth. Revelation 12:11 says believers overcome "by the blood of the Lamb and the word of their testimony." Your testimony—spoken agreement with God's truth—carries eternal power.

Declarations are not about human willpower; they are about echoing what heaven has already spoken.

## CASE STUDY: THE EARLY CHURCH IN PRAYER

In Acts 4, after being threatened, the believers prayed: "Sovereign Lord... consider their threats and enable Your servants to speak Your word with great boldness" (vv. 24, 29).

Their prayer wasn't timid—it aligned with heaven's mission. The result? The place shook, they were filled with the Spirit, and they spoke God's Word boldly. Their participation in heaven's conversation shifted the atmosphere on earth.

## CASE STUDY: ISAIAH'S HEAVENLY VISION

In Isaiah 6, the prophet saw the Lord on His throne, surrounded by seraphim declaring, "Holy, holy, holy." When Isaiah joined the conversation, saying, "Here am I, send me," he stepped into his calling. Your place in the eternal conversation is not passive awe; it is active response.

## LIVING FROM A HEAVENLY SEAT

Being seated with Christ changes your outlook:

1. *Perspective*– From heaven's view, problems shrink and God's sovereignty looms larger.
2. *Authority*– Seated with Christ, you pray and declare from victory, not for victory.
3. *Identity*– You are not a beggar trying to be heard; you are a child invited to the Father's table.
4. *Purpose*– Life is no longer random; every prayer and word contributes to God's kingdom unfolding on earth.

## PRACTICAL WAYS TO PARTNER WITH HEAVEN

1. *Pray Scripture Daily*– Echo God's Word back to Him.
2. *Worship Intentionally*– Make praise your first language.
3. *Declare Boldly*– Speak God's promises over your life, family, and community.
4. *Listen Carefully*– Prayer is not only talking; it's hearing heaven's perspective.
5. *Live With Awareness*– Enter every day conscious that you carry heaven's atmosphere with you.

## ILLUSTRATION: THE COUNCIL CHAMBER

Imagine being invited into a council chamber where the most important decisions are made. You are not there to watch quietly—you are given a voice, a role, and a seat at the table. That's what it means to be seated with Christ. Your life, prayers, and words matter in the unfolding of God's eternal plan.

## ENCOURAGEMENT: YOU BELONG IN THE CONVERSATION

The enemy will try to convince you that your prayers don't matter, your worship is insignificant, or your declarations are powerless. But Scripture says otherwise. You are seated with Christ. You have access to the Father. Your voice is welcomed in heaven's chorus. Never underestimate the power of joining your voice with God's Word.

## PRAYER

Lord, thank You for giving me a seat in Your eternal conversation. Help me live daily with the awareness that I am seated with Christ in heavenly places. Teach me to pray, worship, and declare in agreement with heaven, so that my life reflects Your kingdom on earth. Amen.

## DISCUSSION & REFLECTION

1. How does knowing you are seated with Christ change your outlook on daily life?

_____

_____

_____

_____

_____

2. What practical way can you partner with heaven's conversation this week?

_____

_____

_____

_____

_____

3. Where have you underestimated the power of your prayers or worship?

_____

_____

_____

_____

_____

_____

4. How can you live with greater awareness of your heavenly seat?

_____

_____

_____

_____

_____

_____

# CHAPTER 21
# LIVING FROM A RENEWED MIND

> Do not conform to the pattern of this world, but be transformed by the renewing of your mind. Then you will be able to test and approve what God's will is—His good, pleasing and perfect will.
>
> ROMANS 12:2

E very battle you face—whether spiritual, emotional, or behavioral—has a starting point in the mind. What you believe shapes how you live. This is why Paul emphasized that transformation comes through renewing the mind.

The "pattern of this world" is a system of thinking—fear-driven, self-centered, and opposed to God. To resist it, we must replace it with heaven's perspective. Renewal is not optional for believers—it is essential for walking in God's will.

## THE POWER OF THOUGHT-LIFE

Proverbs 23:7 says, "As a man thinks in his heart, so is he." Thoughts become attitudes. Attitudes shape actions. Actions form habits. Habits establish destiny.

- Negative thinking produces anxiety, bitterness, and defeat.
- Truth-filled thinking produces peace, joy, and endurance.

Your outer life is a reflection of your inner life. To change your life, start by changing your thoughts.

## DAILY RENEWAL, NOT ONE-TIME CHANGE

Romans 12:2 uses the present tense: "be transformed by the renewing of your mind." Renewal is not a one-time event at salvation. It is an ongoing, daily process of alignment.

Just as your body needs daily food, your mind needs daily truth. Without renewal, the noise of culture will conform you to its mold. With renewal, the Spirit transforms you into Christ's likeness.

## CASE STUDY: THE ISRAELITES IN THE WILDERNESS

Though Israel was freed from Egypt, Egypt still lived in their minds. They longed for slavery's food rather than trusting God's promise of freedom. Their lack of renewed thinking kept them wandering.

This illustrates how deliverance without renewal leads to cycles of defeat. God doesn't just want to get you out of Egypt—He wants to get Egypt out of you.

## CASE STUDY: GIDEON'S SHIFT IN MINDSET

When the angel called Gideon a "mighty warrior" (Judges 6:12), Gideon saw himself as weak and insignificant. But as God's Word reshaped his thinking, Gideon acted with courage, and victory followed. Your renewed mind allows you to see yourself as God sees you—chosen, equipped, and victorious.

## CASE STUDY: PAUL'S NEW PERSPECTIVE

Before Christ, Paul's zeal was misdirected, persecuting believers. But after his encounter with Jesus, his renewed mind redefined his mission. He declared, "We take captive every thought to make it obedient to Christ" (2 Corinthians 10:5). Paul's transformation shows the power of a surrendered thought-life.

### Replacing Lies With Truth

The enemy's primary weapon is deception. He whispers lies: "You're not enough. You'll never change. God doesn't care." Renewal means recognizing those lies and replacing them with truth.

**The lie:** "I am worthless."
**The truth:** *"I am God's workmanship."* (Ephesians 2:10)

**The lie:** "I am alone."
**The truth:** *"God will never leave me."* (Hebrews 13:5)

**The lie:** "My past defines me."
**The truth:** *"I am a new creation."* (2 Corinthians 5:17)

Renewal is not just rejecting lies—it's rehearsing truth until it reshapes perspective.

## PRACTICAL HABITS FOR A RENEWED MIND

1. *Daily Scripture Meditation*– Let God's Word fill your mind like oxygen fills your lungs.
2. *Confession of Truth*– Speak promises aloud to reinforce belief.
3. *Prayerful Reflection*– Invite the Spirit to expose lies and replace them with truth.

4. *Gratitude Journaling*– Gratitude shifts focus from lack to God's provision.
5. *Guarding Input*– What you watch, read, and listen to either renews or pollutes your mind.

## ILLUSTRATION: THE COMPUTER RESET

A computer infected with corrupted files runs slowly and erratically. To restore it, you must remove the malware and install updates. Renewal of the mind works the same way—removing toxic thoughts and installing God's truth brings clarity, peace, and function back to your soul.

## LIVING WITH A RENEWED MINDSET

Living from a renewed mind impacts every area of life:

- **Identity** – You see yourself as God's child, not through the lens of failure.
- **Purpose** – You align with kingdom assignment rather than chasing empty pursuits.
- **Relationships** – You respond with love and forgiveness rather than bitterness.
- **Trials** – You view difficulties as opportunities for growth, not reasons for despair.

A renewed mind equips you to discern God's will and walk in it with confidence.

## PRAYER

Spirit of God, renew my mind and align my thoughts with Your Word. Expose every lie I have believed, and replace it with Your eternal truth. Transform me daily until my thinking, speaking, and living reflect Christ. Amen.

## DISCUSSION & REFLECTION

1. What negative thought in your life needs replacing with God's truth?

_____

_____

_____

_____

_____

2. What daily practice can you begin—or strengthen—to renew your mind?

_____

_____

_____

_____

_____

3. How has Scripture meditation or confession of truth shaped your perspective before?

_____

_____

_____

_____

_____

4. Where do you need to surrender thought patterns to the Spirit's renewal today?

_____

_____

_____

_____

_____

_____

# CHAPTER 22
# PRAYER AS PARTICIPATION IN THE CONVERSATION

> This, then, is how you should pray: 'Our Father in heaven, hallowed be Your name, Your kingdom come, Your will be done, on earth as it is in heaven.'
>
> MATTHEW 6:9–10

For many, prayer feels like speaking into the air—listing needs, complaints, or hopes, and then wondering if God heard. But biblical prayer is not a one-sided speech. It is a dialogue. Prayer is entering into heaven's conversation, aligning our hearts with God's will, and listening for His voice as much as we speak.

Jesus modeled this in His life. He often withdrew to lonely places to pray (Luke 5:16). These weren't just moments of reporting needs—they were times of communion, alignment, and listening to the Father.

Prayer is not about informing God of what He doesn't know. He already knows our needs (Matthew 6:8). Prayer is about partnership—joining His eternal conversation so that His kingdom is manifested on earth.

## ALIGNING WITH GOD'S WILL

The Lord's Prayer begins with "Your kingdom come, Your will be done." Prayer is not first about bending God's will to ours, but about bending our will to His.

When we pray, we are tuning our hearts like instruments to heaven's pitch. We learn to want what He wants, to see as He sees, and to move where He leads.

This is why prayer transforms us. We may start with requests, but often we end with surrender. The conversation shifts our perspective, reminding us that His ways are higher than ours (Isaiah 55:8–9).

## INTERCESSION: STANDING IN THE GAP

One of the most profound ways we participate in heaven's conversation is through intercession—praying on behalf of others.

Ezekiel 22:30 says: "I looked for someone among them who would build up the wall and stand before me in the gap on behalf of the land so I would not have to destroy it, but I found no one."

Intercessors are bridge-builders. They stand between heaven and earth, lifting up families, nations, and situations before God, and calling His purposes into those spaces.

## CASE STUDY: ABRAHAM INTERCEDING FOR SODOM

When God revealed His plan to judge Sodom, Abraham stepped into the conversation. He pleaded for mercy, asking if God would spare the city for the sake of the righteous (Genesis 18:22–33). Though the city was destroyed, Abraham's intercession revealed God's openness to dialogue and His heart of mercy. This shows us that prayer is not begging; it is partnership with God's justice and mercy.

## CASE STUDY: MOSES INTERCEDING FOR ISRAEL

After Israel sinned with the golden calf, God spoke of destroying them. But Moses stood in the gap, interceding: "Turn from Your fierce anger; relent and do not bring disaster on Your people" (Exodus 32:12). Scripture says God relented. Prayer has power to move heaven's hand because it aligns with God's heart.

## CASE STUDY: THE EARLY CHURCH AT PRAYER

When Peter was imprisoned, the church gathered and prayed earnestly (Acts 12:5). In response, God sent an angel to free him. Their intercession opened the way for heaven's intervention. This reminds us: prayer is not wasted breath. It is a lifeline of heaven's power into earth's needs.

## LISTENING IN PRAYER

True conversation requires listening. Prayer is not complete until we pause to hear God's response. Elijah discovered that God's voice was not in the wind, earthquake, or fire—but in a gentle whisper (1 Kings 19:12).

The Spirit speaks through Scripture, impressions, peace, dreams, and counsel. When we quiet our hearts, we can hear heaven's side of the conversation.

## THE FRUITS OF A LIFE OF PRAYER

A life of prayer produces:

- **Peace**– Philippians 4:6–7 promises peace that surpasses understanding.
- **Clarity**– Prayer sharpens discernment of God's will.
- **Power**– Prayer releases heaven's resources into earth's battles.

- **Intimacy**– Prayer deepens relationship with God Himself.

## PRACTICAL WAYS TO CULTIVATE A LIFE OF PRAYER

1. *Set a Rhythm*– Choose a time and place daily.
2. *Pray Scripture*– Let God's Word guide your prayers.
3. *Practice Silence*– Create space to listen to the Spirit.
4. *Keep a Prayer Journal*– Record requests and testimonies of answered prayer.
5. *Pray for Others*– Make intercession a regular habit.

## ILLUSTRATION: A HEAVENLY CONFERENCE CALL

Imagine prayer as joining a divine conference call. The Father, Son, and Spirit are already speaking. Angels are worshiping. Saints are interceding. When you pray, you don't start the call—you join it. Your voice adds harmony to the heavenly dialogue.

## LIVING AS A PARTNER IN PRAYER

Prayer is not just a discipline—it is participation. You are not an outsider trying to get God's attention; you are a child already seated with Christ (Ephesians 2:6). Your prayers matter because they are part of God's plan to bring His kingdom to earth.

## PRAYER

Lord, teach me to pray with expectation. Help me not only to speak but also to listen. Align my heart with Your will, and make me a faithful partner in intercession, standing in the gap for others. Amen.

## DISCUSSION & REFLECTION

1. How does prayer shift your perspective when facing challenges?

_____

_____

_____

_____

_____

_____

2. Who is God calling you to intercede for in this season?

_____

_____

_____

_____

_____

_____

3. What practices can help you listen more intentionally in prayer?

_____

_____

_____

_____

_____

_____

4. How might your prayers participate in God's eternal conversation?

_____

_____

_____

_____

_____

_____

## CHAPTER 23
# PROPHETIC PROMISES AND YOUR LIFE

> But the one who prophesies speaks to people for their strengthening, encouraging and comfort.
>
> 1 CORINTHIANS 14:3

From Genesis to Revelation, God is a speaking God. He spoke creation into existence, spoke covenant promises to Abraham, and spoke words of destiny over prophets and kings. In the New Testament, prophecy continued to confirm God's plans and encourage the early church.

Prophecy is not reserved for the Old Testament or for a select few. 1 Corinthians 14 makes clear that prophecy is a gift given to the body of Christ to strengthen, encourage, and comfort. Prophetic promises remind us that God is not silent; He is actively involved in our lives.

## THE PURPOSE OF PROPHECY

Paul outlined three primary purposes of prophecy. Each purpose is listed in 1 Corinthians 14:3:

1. *Strengthening*– Building faith when we feel weak.
2. *Encouragement*– Reminding us of God's presence and promises.
3. *Comfort*– Bringing peace in seasons of pain or uncertainty.

Prophecy is never meant to condemn or shame. It reflects the heart of a Father who guides His children with love.

## CASE STUDY: AGABUS AND PAUL

In Acts 21:10–11, the prophet Agabus warned Paul that imprisonment awaited him in Jerusalem. This prophecy did not deter Paul, but confirmed what God had already prepared his heart for. Prophetic words may not always predict comfort, but they always prepare us with truth and strength.

## CASE STUDY: TIMOTHY'S PROPHETIC ENCOURAGEMENT

Paul reminded Timothy to "fight the battle well" by remembering the prophecies spoken over him (1 Timothy 1:18). Those words anchored Timothy when doubt or fear could have derailed him. Prophetic promises are not just inspiring moments—they are weapons in spiritual warfare, reminders to persevere in faith.

## TESTING PROPHETIC WORDS

Scripture also teaches discernment. Not every word spoken in God's name is from Him. 1 Thessalonians 5:20–21 says: "Do not treat prophecies with contempt but test them all; hold on to what is good."

Ways to test prophecy:

- Does it align with Scripture? God never contradicts His Word.

- Does it glorify Jesus? Revelation 19:10 says the testimony of Jesus is the spirit of prophecy.
- Is it confirmed in community? Wise counsel and spiritual leaders help discern.
- Does it bear fruit of peace, encouragement, and clarity? God is not the author of confusion.

## STEWARDING PROPHETIC PROMISES

Receiving a prophetic word is only the beginning. Stewardship means holding it with care, testing it with wisdom, and praying it into reality.

Practical ways to steward:

1. *Record It*– Write it down or keep it in a journal.
2. *Pray Over It*– Ask God to clarify timing and application.
3. **Submit It to Counsel**– Share with trusted leaders or mentors.
4. *Align With It*– Take practical steps of obedience when confirmed.
5. *Hold It Loosely*– Trust God's timing, not human deadlines.

## PROPHECY AS PARTNERSHIP

Prophetic words are not automatic guarantees—they are invitations to faith. Like seeds, they must be watered with prayer, patience, and obedience. Hebrews 6:12 reminds us that we inherit promises "through faith and patience." When stewarded well, prophecy builds endurance and direction for the journey.

## ILLUSTRATION: A COMPASS, NOT A MAP

Prophecy is like a compass. It points you in a direction, but it doesn't give every detail of the journey. God may reveal glimpses of the destination while still requiring you to walk in daily trust. This keeps us dependent on Him rather than on the prophecy itself.

## ENCOURAGEMENT FOR THE WEARY

Maybe you've received prophetic promises that haven't yet come to pass. Do not lose heart. Joseph received dreams of leadership long before they were fulfilled—and the path included betrayal, prison, and waiting. Delay is not denial. Steward the word, remain faithful, and trust that God's timing is perfect.

## PRAYER

Lord, help me to treasure prophetic promises, testing them with wisdom and holding fast to what is good. Give me discernment to recognize Your voice, faith to believe Your Word, and patience to walk in alignment with Your timing. Amen.

## DISCUSSION & REFLECTION

1. What prophetic promise has encouraged you in your faith journey?

_____
_____
_____
_____
_____

2. How can you steward words spoken over your life with wisdom and accountability?

_____
_____
_____
_____
_____
_____

3. Where do you need renewed patience for promises not yet fulfilled?

_____
_____
_____
_____
_____
_____

4. Who in your community can help you test and confirm prophetic words?

_____
_____
_____
_____
_____
_____

# CHAPTER 24
# COMMUNITY AND THE CONVERSATION

> While they were worshiping the Lord and fasting, the Holy Spirit said, 'Set apart for Me Barnabas and Saul for the work to which I have called them.' So after they had fasted and prayed, they placed their hands on them and sent them off.
>
> ACTS 13:2–3

Many of us imagine hearing God as a solitary pursuit—a quiet place, a Bible, and a whispered prayer. While intimacy with God in the secret place is essential, Scripture also shows that God often speaks in community.

In Acts 13, the church in Antioch gathered to worship and fast together. It was in that shared atmosphere that the Holy Spirit spoke, calling Paul and Barnabas into their missionary assignment. The Spirit chose to reveal His will not in private isolation but in the context of community.

God's eternal conversation is not only vertical—between Him and you—but also horizontal, flowing through brothers and sisters in Christ.

## THE POWER OF SHARED DISCERNMENT

When we walk alone, our perspective can be limited. We may misinterpret God's voice through our own desires, fears, or biases. But in community, God provides confirmation and clarity.

Proverbs 11:14 says: "Where there is no guidance, a people falls, but in an abundance of counselors there is safety."

The body of Christ was designed for mutual discernment. Together, we are sharper, wiser, and stronger.

## CONFESSION AND HEALING IN COMMUNITY

James 5:16 teaches: "Therefore confess your sins to each other and pray for each other so that you may be healed."

Confession is not about shame—it is about freedom. In community, secrets lose their power and grace flows. Healing often comes not in isolation but in the safety of trusted fellowship.

## ENCOURAGEMENT AS PROPHETIC FUEL

Hebrews 10:24–25 says: "Let us consider how we may spur one another on toward love and good deeds, not giving up meeting together... but encouraging one another."

Encouragement is not a casual pat on the back—it is fuel for perseverance. God often uses the voices of others to remind us of His promises when our own faith grows weak.

## CASE STUDY: MOSES AND AARON

When God called Moses, Moses felt inadequate. God responded by sending Aaron to speak alongside him (Exodus 4:14–16). Community strengthened Moses' obedience. Sometimes, God answers our fears not by removing us from the call but by surrounding us with people who will walk beside us.

## CASE STUDY: RUTH AND NAOMI

Ruth's loyalty to Naomi forged a bond that would change history. By walking together, they stepped into God's redemption story, leading to the lineage of King David and ultimately Jesus. Community doesn't just confirm God's voice—it multiplies legacy.

## CASE STUDY: THE EARLY CHURCH IN ACTS

The first believers devoted themselves to teaching, fellowship, breaking bread, and prayer (Acts 2:42). Their unity created an atmosphere where God's power flowed, needs were met, and the gospel spread rapidly. Community was not optional; it was the very environment of God's conversation.

## OBSTACLES TO COMMUNITY

1. *Isolation*– Believing we can do faith alone
2. *Offense*– Allowing hurt to separate us from fellowship
3. *Pride*– Thinking we don't need others' counsel or encouragement
4. *Busyness*– Neglecting community for convenience

But the truth is clear: God designed us for each other. Faith flourishes in fellowship.

## PRACTICAL WAYS TO DEEPEN FELLOWSHIP

1. *Commit to a Local Church*– Community requires consistency.
2. *Seek Counsel*– Invite trusted believers to speak into your decisions.
3. *Practice Confession*– Share struggles with safe people who will pray.

4. *Encourage Regularly*– Be intentional about speaking life to others.
5. *Pray Together*– Join in corporate prayer, aligning with heaven as one body.

## ILLUSTRATION: THE CHOIR VS. THE SOLOIST

A soloist can sing beautifully, but a choir carries a fullness and harmony one voice cannot create. God designed His conversation to be a choir, not a solo. When the body of Christ lifts its voice together, heaven's song resounds with power.

## LIVING IN HEAVEN'S FAMILY

To live in community is to live as part of God's family. You are not an orphan, wandering alone. You are a son or daughter seated with Christ among brothers and sisters.

Community is where your gifts are sharpened, your calling is confirmed, and your heart is encouraged. It is where heaven's conversation becomes visible on earth.

## PRAYER

Lord, root me in community where Your voice is confirmed and celebrated. Give me courage to confess, humility to listen, and boldness to encourage. Let my life reflect the beauty of Your family on earth. Amen.

## DISCUSSION & REFLECTION

1. How has God spoken to you through others in your community?

_____

_____

_____

_____

_____

2. What steps can you take to deepen your fellowship with other believers?

_____

_____

_____

_____

_____

3. Are there relationships in your community that need reconciliation or renewal?

_____

_____

_____

_____

_____

4. How can you encourage someone in your church or small group this week?

_____

_____

_____

_____

_____

_____

# CHAPTER 25
# A LIFESTYLE WRAPPED IN THE WORD

> Being confident of this, that He who began a good work in you will carry it on to completion until the day of Christ Jesus.
>
> PHILIPPIANS 1:6

Living in God's conversation is not a single event, an inspiring service, or an occasional breakthrough. It is a lifestyle—a daily surrender to His Word, His Spirit, and His will. To be wrapped in God's Word is to let His truth cover, guide, and shape every part of your life.

Like clothing you put on every day, God's Word is not meant to be taken off and on depending on mood or circumstance. Colossians 3:16 says: "Let the word of Christ dwell in you richly."

Richly means abundantly, consistently, and deeply. To live wrapped in the Word is to live in constant awareness of His truth.

## DAILY SURRENDER

A lifestyle wrapped in the Word begins each day with surrender. Jesus modeled this in John 5:19: "The Son can do nothing by Himself; He can do only what He sees His Father doing."

If Jesus lived in daily dependence on the Father, how much more must we? Each morning becomes a conversation starter: "Lord, not my will, but Yours be done today." Surrender is not defeat. It is alignment with the One who knows best.

## GOD'S ONGOING WORK IN YOU

Philippians 1:6 reminds us that God is not finished. The conversation continues. Every season, every chapter of your life, is part of His unfolding story.

- In youth, He speaks identity.
- In trial, He speaks faithfulness.
- In maturity, He speaks legacy.

From beginning to end, He is completing the good work He began. Living wrapped in the Word means trusting the process, even when the outcome is unseen.

## CASE STUDY: JOSHUA'S LIFELONG OBEDIENCE

Joshua was commanded: "Keep this Book of the Law always on your lips; meditate on it day and night." (Joshua 1:8). His leadership and victories flowed from a lifestyle wrapped in God's Word. Joshua's success was not about charisma or strategy but about consistent obedience to God's conversation.

## CASE STUDY: MARY'S LIFELONG "YES"

When the angel spoke God's Word to Mary, she replied: "Let it be to me according to your word." (Luke 1:38). That yes wrapped her life in God's purposes. From Bethlehem to the cross, Mary lived surrendered to the Word spoken over her. Her story reminds us that a lifestyle wrapped in the Word is not easy but always fruitful.

## CASE STUDY: PAUL'S LIFELONG PURSUIT

Paul, near the end of his life, declared: "I have fought the good fight, I have finished the race, I have kept the faith." (2 Timothy 4:7). His life was wrapped in God's Word from the Damascus road to his final letters. He lived in constant discipleship, knowing God's conversation was not finished until eternity.

## RHYTHMS OF A WORD-WRAPPED LIFE

1. *Scripture Reading and Meditation*– Not as a checklist, but as communion with God's voice.
2. *Prayer and Worship*– Talking and listening daily to the One who speaks.
3. *Community Fellowship*– Surrounding yourself with voices that confirm and encourage God's Word.
4. *Obedience in Action*– Living the Word, not just hearing it (James 1:22).
5. *Reflection and Gratitude*– Journaling testimonies of God's conversation in your life.

## ILLUSTRATION: THE VINE AND THE BRANCHES

Jesus said in John 15:5: "I am the vine; you are the branches. If you remain in Me and I in you, you will bear much fruit; apart from Me you can do nothing."

Living wrapped in the Word is remaining in Him—staying connected, nourished, and dependent. Just as a branch cannot thrive apart from the vine, our lives cannot flourish apart from His ongoing conversation.

## ENCOURAGING OTHERS INTO THE LIFESTYLE

Your lifestyle becomes a witness. When others see you consistently wrapped in God's Word—responding with peace in crisis, joy in hardship, and faith in uncertainty—they are drawn to the same source. Encouraging others doesn't always mean preaching; it often looks like modeling. People are inspired by lived faith.

## THE ETERNAL PERSPECTIVE

A life wrapped in the Word is preparation for eternity. The conversations we nurture now are rehearsals for the eternal dialogue in heaven, where saints and angels forever declare God's glory. Your discipleship on earth prepares you for your destiny in eternity—to live forever in the presence and Word of God.

## PRAYER

Lord, wrap my life in Your Word. Let every thought, word, and action reflect Your promises and purposes. Thank You for completing the good work You began in me. May my lifestyle of surrender draw others into Your eternal conversation. Amen.

## DISCUSSION & REFLECTION

1. What new rhythms can you practice to stay wrapped in God's Word daily?

_____

_____

_____

_____

_____

2. How can you encourage friends, family, or community to live this lifestyle with you?

_____

_____

_____

_____

_____

3. Where do you see evidence that God is still completing His work in your life?

_____

_____

_____

_____

_____

_____

4. What does it mean to you personally to live "wrapped" in His promises and purposes?

_____

_____

_____

_____

_____

# ECHOING HEAVEN'S CONVERSATION

> For the Lord is good and His love endures forever; His faithfulness continues through all generations.
>
> PSALM 100:5

A s we come to the close of this journey, let us pause and remember the truth woven through every chapter: you are loved, you are chosen, and you are called.

Before you ever spoke a word, God had already spoken one over you. Before you took your first breath, He declared purpose, identity, and destiny for your life. The eternal conversation of heaven has always included you.

This is not wishful thinking—it is Scripture. Ephesians 1:4 declares: "For He chose us in Him before the creation of the world to be holy and blameless in His sight."

You were chosen before you were born. Loved before you could love Him back. Called before you knew His name.

## HEAVEN'S SONG OVER YOU

Zephaniah 3:17 paints a stunning picture: "The Lord your God is with you, the Mighty Warrior who saves. He will take great delight in you; in His love He will no longer rebuke you, but will rejoice over you with singing."

Heaven is not silent. Over your life, God is singing. His song is one of delight, hope, and promise. When you step into prayer, worship, and declaration, you are not starting something new—you are joining a song that has been playing since before the foundations of the world.

## WALKING DAILY IN AGREEMENT

The greatest response you can give to heaven's conversation is to live in agreement with it. Agreement looks like:

- Believing God's Word even when feelings say otherwise.
- Speaking His promises even when circumstances disagree.
- Acting in faith even when you cannot see the outcome.
- Trusting His timing even when waiting feels unbearable.

Walking daily in agreement is not about perfection—it is about posture. It is the choice, again and again, to align your heart, words, and actions with the Father's voice.

## GOD'S PURPOSES WILL STAND

Life is filled with uncertainty. Plans change. People disappoint. Circumstances shift. But God's purposes never fail. Isaiah 46:10 reminds us: "My purpose will stand, and I will do all that I please."

This means you can rest secure. No failure is final when you walk with the God of redemption. No obstacle can overturn what He has ordained. No trial can silence His promises over your life.

## LIVING AS A MESSENGER OF HEAVEN

Your life is not just about receiving God's conversation—it is about becoming part of it. Every time you pray, worship, encourage, forgive, or declare His Word, you release heaven's reality into earth.

You are not just a listener—you are a messenger. You carry heaven's language into your family, workplace, neighborhood, and generation.

## ILLUSTRATION: THE ECHO OF ETERNITY

Imagine standing at the base of a mountain. You shout, and your voice echoes back again and again. In the same way, when you join your voice with heaven, the sound doesn't end with you. It reverberates across generations, echoing into eternity.

Your words, your prayers, your worship—they do not vanish. They join the eternal conversation of heaven, carrying weight far beyond what you see.

## AN ONGOING JOURNEY

This book may be ending, but your journey is not. Every day is another page in the story God is writing with your life. Every moment is another opportunity to tune in, to listen, and to respond.

- *Chapter 1* reminded you: God speaks about you.
- *Chapter 2* revealed: Jesus is your Mediator.
- *Chapter 3* showed: the Spirit reveals God's thoughts.
- *Chapter 4* reminded us: angels and witnesses are engaged.
- *Chapter 5* grounded us in Scripture as heaven's record.
- *Chapters 6–15* guided us in identity, purpose, destiny, relationships, finances, and legacy.
- *Chapters 16–24* revealed the power of your words, prayers, and community.

- And in *Chapter 25*, we embraced the call to live wrapped in God's Word.

Each chapter has been a doorway into a greater reality: you are part of heaven's ongoing conversation.

# A FINAL EXHORTATION

*Beloved child of God, never forget:*

- You are loved deeply.
- You are chosen intentionally.
- You are called eternally.

Your Father's voice is not distant. His conversation is near, alive, and unbroken. Heaven is filled with His promises, and you are seated with Christ in that eternal dialogue.

So walk boldly. Pray faithfully. Speak truth courageously. Love generously. Endure trials patiently. Worship joyfully. And above all—live wrapped in the Word.

For the One who began a good work in you will be faithful to complete it.

## PRAYER

Lord, seal Your Word in my heart and let my life echo heaven's conversation. Thank You that I am loved, chosen, and called according to Your eternal purpose. May my words, actions, and thoughts align with Your will, and may my life leave a legacy that reflects Your kingdom. Amen.

# ACKNOWLEDGMENTS

Writing a book is never a solo journey. Though the words on these pages carry my name, they have been shaped, inspired, and supported by many others.

*First, I give thanks to God,* the Author of life and the One whose eternal Word is the true foundation of this work. Without His voice, there would be no conversation to share.

*To my family*—thank you for your love, patience, and encouragement throughout this process. Your prayers and unwavering belief in me gave me strength on the days I needed it most.

*To my church family and community of faith*—you have been living testimonies of God's goodness and grace. Your fellowship and encouragement remind me daily of the beauty of walking together in the Word.

*To the friends and mentors who challenged me,* prayed for me, and reminded me to stay faithful to the vision—this book carries your fingerprints as much as mine.

*And finally, to you, the reader*—thank you for opening these pages and allowing me to walk alongside you. My prayer is that you will not only read these words but also hear God's voice speaking directly to your heart.

# ABOUT THE AUTHOR

**Dr. Tony Medley Sr.** is a pastor, teacher, mentor, and author whose life and ministry have been dedicated to helping people discover the power of God's Word spoken over their lives. Known for his passionate preaching and practical teaching, Dr. Medley has spent decades equipping believers to hear God's voice, walk in their identity in Christ, and live with purpose and bold faith.

His ministry extends beyond the pulpit—through books, training materials, stage plays, and discipleship resources—designed to ignite transformation in individuals, churches, and communities. Dr. Medley combines deep biblical insight with everyday application, ensuring that readers not only understand the Scriptures but also live them out with confidence.

With a message that is both prophetic and practical, Dr. Medley inspires people to see themselves through heaven's perspective. He believes every person is "wrapped in the conversation" of God and destined to thrive in His promises.

When he is not writing or teaching, Dr. Medley is serving his church family, mentoring emerging leaders, and enjoying time with his own family, who remain his greatest earthly joy.

www.ingramcontent.com/pod-product-compliance
Lightning Source LLC
Chambersburg PA
CBHW051519120626
46551CB00012B/986